T0184814

Zero Trust Journey Across the Digital Estate

Today's organizations require a new security approach that effectively adapts to the challenges of the modern environment, embraces the mobile workforce, and protects people, devices, apps, and data wherever they are located. Zero Trust is increasingly becoming the critical security approach of choice for many enterprises and governments; however, security leaders often struggle with the significant shifts in strategy and architecture required to holistically implement Zero Trust.

This book seeks to provide an end-to-end view of the Zero Trust approach across organizations' digital estates that includes strategy, business imperatives, architecture, solutions, human elements, implementation approaches, that could significantly benefit them to learn, adapt, and implement Zero Trust. The book concludes with a discussion of the future of Zero Trust in areas such as artificial intelligence, blockchain technology, operational technology (OT), and governance, risk, and compliance.

The book is ideal for business decision makers, cybersecurity leaders, security technical professionals, and organizational change agents who want to modernize their digital estate with the Zero Trust approach.

Zero Trust Journey Across the Digital Estate

Abbas Kudrati and Binil Pillai

CRC Press
Taylor & Francis Group
Boca Raton London

CRC Press is an imprint of the
Taylor & Francis Group, an **informa** business

First edition published 2023
by CRC Press
6000 Broken Sound Parkway NW, Suite 300, Boca Raton, FL
33487–2742

and by CRC Press
4 Park Square, Milton Park, Abingdon, Oxon, OX14 4RN

CRC Press is an imprint of Taylor & Francis Group, LLC

© 2023 Abbas Kudrati and Binil Pillai

Library of Congress Cataloging-in-Publication Data
Names: Pillai, Binil, author. | Kudrati, Abbas, author.
Title: Zero trust journey across the digital estate / Binil A. Pillai,
    Abbas S. Kudrati.
Description: First edition. | Boca Raton : CRC Press, [2022] |
    Includes bibliographical references and index. | Identifiers:
    LCCN 2022002002 (print) | LCCN 2022002003 (ebook) |
    ISBN 9781032125480 (hbk) | ISBN 9781032125497 (pbk) |
    ISBN 9781003225096 (ebk)
Subjects: LCSH: Computer networks—Security measures. | Business
    information services—Security measures. | Computer security.
Classification: LCC TK5105.59 .P597 2022 (print) |
    LCC TK5105.59 (ebook) | DDC 005.8—dc23/eng/20220408
LC record available at https://lccn.loc.gov/2022002002
LC ebook record available at https://lccn.loc.gov/2022002003

ISBN: 978-1-032-12548-0 (hbk)
ISBN: 978-1-032-12549-7 (pbk)
ISBN: 978-1-003-22509-6 (ebk)

DOI: 10.1201/9781003225096

Typeset in Sabon
by Apex CoVantage, LLC

I dedicate this book to my beloved wife, Fatema; my son, Murtaza; and my daughter, Batool, whom I "trust explicitly," and that trust requires "no implicit verification".

—Abbas Kudrati

I dedicate this book to my life partner, Dhanya Ramakrishnan, not only for her love and care but also for her constant warmth and companionship that I cannot repay even with a lifetime.

—Binil Pillai

Contents

Author Biographies

Abbas Kudrati, a long-time cybersecurity practitioner and CISO, is Microsoft Asia's Chief Cybersecurity Advisor. Abbas works with customers on cybersecurity strategy, how Microsoft sees the threat landscape, how we are investing in the future of security at Microsoft, and how organizations can take advantage of Microsoft's security solutions to help improve their security posture and reduce costs.

In addition to his work at Microsoft, he serves as an executive advisor to Deakin University, LaTrobe University, HITRUST ASIA, EC Council ASIA, and many security and technology startups. He supports the broader security community through his work with ISACA chapters and student mentorship. He is also a part-time professor at LaTrobe University, Melbourne, Australia, and a regular speaker on Zero Trust, cybersecurity, cloud security, governance, risk, and compliance.

Abbas has received multiple industry awards, such as Business Leader/Professional of the year 2021 by IABCA, Top Security Advisor for APJ for the years 2019 and 2020, Best Security Professional of the year 2018, CISO 100 Award 2018, Finalist for Australian CISO of the year 2015, IT Governance Professional of the year 2014, and Security Strategist of the year 2011.

He is the bestselling author of books such as *"Threat Hunting in the Cloud"* and *"Digitization Risks in Post Pandemic World."*

He graduated from Gujarat University, India, with a bachelor's degree in accounting and auditing and is a certified Forrester Zero Trust Strategist, C|CISO, CISM, CISA, CGEIT, CPDSE, and CSX-P, among other professional certifications.

Binil Pillai is a strategic-thinking business development professional with 23 years of multifaceted experience building relationships, cultivating partnerships, retaining customers, and growing profit channels by establishing trust. As Global Director of Security, Compliance and Identity business at Microsoft, Binil is responsible for strategy and business development and works with corporate executives and partners to evangelize security as a foundational capability to accelerate a secure digital transformation journey for customers. Binil has experience in security product development, has managed security product marketing, and has led worldwide security go-to-market and sales activations. He was the business architect who designed and launched the Business Value Analysis model to quantify security risk exposure for B2B customers. Before joining Microsoft, Binil worked as a regional practice manager for Deloitte Consulting's strategy and operations practice. His business strategy consulting experience spans business transformation, corporate strategy alignment, post-merger integration, adoption and change management, customer relationship management, IT strategic planning, and more, with a wide range of companies and government agencies. He is also a board adviser to several start-ups to help grow their business successfully.

Binil is passionate about establishing a coaching culture to improve learning and performance, make the most of the people's potential and deliver sustainable results. As a PROCI-certified change management practitioner, Binil embraces the leadership accountability to take a step-by-step approach that helps the organization achieve success, no matter how complex the system, process, method, or culture need to affect or transform. Binil graduated from INSEAD in Business Strategy & Financial Acumen and has a master's in business administration. He is TOGAF certified enterprise architect and account-based marketing professional from ITSMA.

He has also published a book for Wiley (*Threat Hunting in the Cloud: Defending AWS, Azure and Other Platforms Against Cyberattacks*) and many thought leadership documents. His recent publication is "*How COVID-19 Changes Small Medium Enterprise (SME) Priority on Security.*"

Technical Editor Biography

David Fairman is an experienced CSO/CISO, strategic advisory, investor, and coach. David has extensive experience in the global financial services sector. David is currently the APAC CIO & CSO for Netskope helping customers manage their digital and cyber risk programs in addition to working across industry with the aim of making the digital economy a safer place to do business. Furthermore, David is a partner and CISO-in-residence at SixThirty Ventures, driving innovation and helping build great technology companies. Previously, David was the chief security officer at NAB owning all aspects of physical security, fraud, investigations, and cyber security. Prior to NAB, he was the group chief information security officer (CISO) for the Royal Bank of Canada. David has been a senior leader at JP Morgan Chase & Co as Deputy Technology Controls Officer and Global Head of Technology Risk and Control. David has also held several senior roles at the Royal Bank of Scotland, including CISO RBS Americas and Head of Information Security EMEA.

David has lived and worked in Australia, the United Kingdom, the Netherlands, and the United States. David was raised and educated in Australia, where he received his bachelor of information technology in software engineering and computer science. He holds a Master of Business Administration and a Master of Project Management. David began his career in Information Security while serving in the Royal Australian Air Force's Electronic Warfare and Communications group, where he gained valuable experience in the technology, policy, and process aspects of security and risk management. Subsequently, David worked in a variety of roles in technology and cyber, including in the utilities sector (gas and electricity). David holds a number of positions on boards of directors and was a founding member of the Security Advisor Alliance (www.securityadvisoralliance.org) and the Canadian Cyber Threat Exchange. During his tenure at NAB, David was the chair for the Board of Directors for the Australian Financial Crimes Exchange and spearheaded the formation of a taskforce involving the big four banks, AFP, ASD, and ACSC to detect and disrupt cyber crime impacting Australia. David also advises several VC funds and Cyber Security companies. Recently, David was recognized in the Top 50 Australian Professionals, as profiled by *Top 100 Magazine*. David has also been named as one of the Top 10 CISOs to know and is recognized as a thought leader in the cyber security industry as profiled by K-Logix. David co-authored *Cyber Risk* (2016) and co-edited *Fintech: Growth and Deregulation* (2018) published by Risk Books. David is passionate about education. He has held adjunct professorships at both the University of New York and the University of Toronto and is currently working with Deakin University in Australia. David currently resides in both Melbourne and Brisbane, Australia.

Foreword

I am honored to lead Microsoft 365 Security, the team responsible for building critical products across the Microsoft Defender family, specifically chartered with keeping so many customers, employees, and users safe. Over the past six years, I have watched ever-increasing investment from both Microsoft and companies across the technology industry as we wrestle with the core problem of making sure that organizations of all sizes and shapes stay productive and secure. It is not news to anyone in security, or even technology more broadly, that this work happens in the face of ever-increasing attacks.

As we deal with this critical problem, it is essential that we stay focused on the critical goal: the needs of customers and their businesses. In short, it does no good to build technology castles in the sky without grounding them in the real needs of real organizations.

In this context, I have been delighted to work with both Abbas Kudrati and Binil Pillai. I have had the pleasure of working with them in multiple customer engagements and see two critical things. First, we share an underlying enthusiasm for the potential of technology to solve challenging problems. I saw this in their recently published book called *Threat Hunting in the Cloud*, which digs into the details of how advanced security technology can help solve previously unapproachable problems. Second, they have demonstrated amazing dedication to making a real difference for customers and security practitioners by deeply understanding the complexity and challenges of cybersecurity for a range of organizations.

For any practitioner in the security industry or indeed most folks involved in technology in any way, the current cybersecurity trends are clear: attacks are increasing every year. As technology brings the world closer together and constantly decreases any friction, it makes it easier for all kinds of attackers to engage in nefarious activities. This is true for advanced nation-state adversaries and for all of the criminal cyber organizations engaged in fraud, ransomware attacks, or even just criminal mischief. Unfortunately, these attackers are taking advantage of new technology and learning new attack techniques at an ever-increasing rate. We need to shift the game for any organization trying to defend itself against this. We need to break away from the mindset that we can build perfect walls to keep attackers out; instead, we need to think deeply about how the strategy, posture, policy, people, and configuration of a digital estate drive great defense.

This is precisely where Zero Trust comes in: a toolset and framework to think about security defense in a modern world. And this is exactly where the book that you hold in your hands will be most useful because it provides a broad view and understanding of what Zero Trust means and how it disrupts the business model now and in the future.

Abbas Kudrati and Binil Pillai are able to leverage their, strategic thinking, business acumen, diverse customer experience, deep technical expertise, and breadth to bear to provide both a broad overview as well as detailed pragmatic steps. This is critical because, from the outside, Zero Trust can be daunting, raising multiple questions of "How do I get started?" "Where am I now?" and "What is my most important next step?" But Abbas Kudrati and Binil Pillai apply their extensive expertise and deep understanding of customers, to make this tractable by breaking down what happens with real customers and real case studies. Again, this application of real-world knowledge and experience makes their insights so valuable.

If we are going to change the game on attackers and think differently, then we need to think about Zero Trust as a journey. There is no "one magical thing" that will fix an entire organization's security problems. Instead, there can only be a constant and dedicated focus on mastering the real complexity that we see in customer estates every day. And as with all journeys, you have to take the ever-important first step. "Zero Trust journey across your Digital Estate" is that essential first step for your journey. Whether you are a CISO who want to explain the value of Zero Trust architecture to the senior management or a security practitioner who want to adopt the best practices of Zero Trust, there is something here to help you bring your organization to a robust security posture.

Rob Lefferts
Corporate Vice President
Microsoft Corporation

Acknowledgment

As cybersecurity professionals, we believe writing a book about Zero Trust is a most needed responsibility to the current time. Although Zero Trust is one of the most frequently discussed topics in the cybersecurity world and at the same time, there is an opportunity to simplify the explanation of the Zero Trust concept across an organization's digital estate that could significantly benefit large, small, and medium enterprises that want to learn to adapt and implement Zero Trust model.

We recognize many people who have influenced our professional lives and our thinking over the past 20 years and more.

It has been our pleasure to work with **David Fairman** (Asia Pacific CIO & CSO – Netskope) as technical editor. He has not only performed technical review responsibilities but also contributed content in a few chapters. As an experienced CISO, his guidance and contributions were remarkable in shaping the book structure.

A special thanks to **Gabriella Williams**, Editor at CRC Press, our main point of contact since the proposal submission. Thanks, Gabby, for professionally walking us through the process and providing guidance, diligence, flexibility, and patience in managing us from different time zones.

This book would not be possible without some other key contributions.

Nigel Wyatt for his initial screening of our proposal, and guidance on the publishing options, and most important, connecting us with Gabriella Williams from CRC Press.

We are immensely grateful to get Foreword from **Rob Lefferts**, Corporate Vice President, Microsoft Corporation. Thanks to your guidance and support.

We owe an enormous debt of gratitude to **Dr. Chase Cunningham** (aka Dr. Zero Trust), who gave us detailed and constructive comments about our book. We are thrilled to have him on board with this project.

This book wouldn't have been possible without leveraging well-articulated Zero Trust concepts and models from corporate organizations – **Microsoft, Netskope, ZScaller,** and **SilverFort** – that allowed us to develop insightful content.

We would also like extended our thanks to **Associate Professor William Yeoh** and **Marina Liu** from Deakin University, Australia for their generous contribution to the development of the "Zero Trust Maturity Assessment Tool" which is published as part of this book.

Special thanks to **Mark Simos** (Principal Partner Tech Architect – Microsoft), **Micah Heaton** (Director, Microsoft Security Solutions – BlueVoyant), **Vik Verma** (Zero Trust Global Blackbelt Microsoft), **Avinash Patney** (Senior Consultant – Microsoft), **Yiftach Keshet** (Director of Product Marketing – Silverfort), **Brett James** (Director, Transformation Strategy at Zscaler), and **Tony Jarvis** (Director, Enterprise Security – Darktrace) for sharing valuable insights to help us develop our content.

Last but not least, we thank our respective family members for their support throughout the authoring process.

Abbas Kudrati and Binil Pillai

Introduction

The continued rise in cyberattacks and ransomware has awakened business leaders worldwide to a new reality. The threats to network and data security have grown beyond what many traditional security solutions can defend against. Zero Trust is a proactive, integrated approach to security across all layers of the digital estate that explicitly and continuously verifies every transaction, asserts the least privilege, and relies on intelligence, advanced detection, and real-time response to threats. Zero Trust is one of the most effective ways for organizations to control access to their networks, applications, and data.

The global Zero Trust security market size is expected to reach US$59.43 billion by 2028, registering a Compound Annual Growth Rate (CAGR) of 15.2% from 2021 to 2028, according to a new study conducted by Grand View Research, Inc. The market is driven by the need to protect enterprise digital environments by averting lateral movement, leveraging network segmentation, simplifying granular user-access control, and implementing layer 7 threat prevention. The robust solutions for implementing a Zero Trust security environment ensure the protection of computers, programs, and networks from unauthorized access. Moreover, preventing unwarranted access to critical data, as the adoption of technologies, such as cloud computing, Wi-Fi, and Internet of Things (IoT), coupled with increasing outsourcing service, is driving the growth of the market. The COVID-19 pandemic has further acted as a catalyst for market growth with enterprises investing in securing their networks, endpoints, and information technology (IT) infrastructure with a Zero Trust security framework.

When organizations adopt a Zero Trust strategy, beyond protecting valuable data by reducing the chance of a breach, there's also a bottom-line benefit. Studies have shown that Zero Trust approaches result in 50% fewer breaches and that companies spend 40% less on technology because all technologies are integrated. In addition, according to a recent Forrester study, companies that adopted Zero Trust were twice as confident in their ability to bring new business models and customer experiences to the market. Preventing attacks is excellent but making products and experiences that customers love is what makes a company great.

DOI: 10.1201/9781003225096-1

The cloud deployment model of Zero Trust security solutions benefits enterprises with cloud-based solutions offering speed, scalability, and enhanced IT security. As more applications get deployed over the cloud, there is a growing demand for cloud-based Zero Trust security solutions among small medium enterprises and large enterprises. By organization size, the large enterprise segment is expected to hold a larger market. By region, North America is expected to account for the largest market share during the forecast period.

We hear some practical questions from customers and technology implementation partners daily when adopting the Zero Trust architecture (ZTA) to minimize security risk exposure and expedite the digital transformation journey. We have made our best effort to address some of the critical questions throughout this book

- What are the current driving forces of ZTA in today's rapidly changing environment?
- Why should business leaders care about Zero Trust?
- How does Zero Trust disrupt the business model today and in the future?
- What are some of the top industry leading ZTA models and standards that organizations can consider for Zero Trust architecture?
- When it comes to network access, why do we think Zero Trust starts with a default deny posture for everyone – government, enterprises, small businesses, and consumers?
- As remote work becomes a new normal, how do Zero Trust principles help maintain security amid the IT complexity of hybrid work?
- What is the relevance of organizational culture for the successful adoption of Zero Trust?
- What are the human elements by role in successfully adopting ZTA?
- How does the future horizon look like for Zero Trust?

What Is Unique about This Book?

Today, technology leaders need a security model that can effectively adapt to the complexity of the modern environment, embraces the mobile workforce; and protects people, devices, apps, and data wherever they're located. Zero Trust is rapidly becoming the security model of choice for many organizations; however, security leaders often struggle with the significant shifts in strategy and architecture required to implement Zero Trust holistically.

This book provides an end-to-end view of the Zero Trust approach across organization's digital estates that includes strategy, business imperatives, architecture, solutions, human elements, and implementation approach that could significantly benefit large, small, and medium enterprises that want to learn adapt and implement Zero Trust.

The book's scope is primarily benefited for business decision makers, security leadership, and organizational change agents who want to adopt and implement the Zero Trust model across their digital estate.

Readers will be in a better position to strategize, plan, and design a credible and defensible Zero Trust security architecture and solution for their organization, understand the relevance of human elements, and learn the best practices from the use cases we included and implement a stepwise journey that delivers significantly improved security and streamlined operations. The book also provides clarity about how Zero Trust model will continue to evolve.

A number of key technology players today offer Zero Trust Security solutions to cater to the demands and needs of the market. Microsoft, Google, AWS, Netskope, Citrix, Cisco Systems, Akamai Technologies, Palo Alto Networks, Symantec Corporation, Okta, Forcepoint, VMware, Cloudflare, IBM Corporation, Fortinet, and Check Point Software Technologies are few of the vendors among many. Any organizations that embrace the above key players' security products also require better guidance for reference and implementation. We believe this book fills that gap to adopt the best practices and align with future trends.

We have structured the book into three parts:

- **Part 1** – What is Zero Trust, how it all started, why business and technology leaders need to adopt this new model. In Part 1 of this book, three chapters provide the historical overview of the Zero Trust concept. We have also provided some of the most commonly used Zero Trust framework and standards, which can be adopted based on your organization's needs and preferences.
- **Part 2** – What is my current status to start my Zero Trust journey? How do I assess my organization's maturity? In Part 2 of this book, we introduce a practical and straightforward maturity model that can evaluate your current organization posture against any Zero Trust framework; we have also provided architecture and implementation details for all the Zero Trust components and executable and straightforward project plan.
- **Part 3** – What next? In Part 3 of this book, you will read about the future horizon of Zero Trust relative to a few emerging and disruptive technologies such as the IoT, artificial intelligence (AI), machine language, blockchain technology, and so on.

Here is a further breakdown of chapter contents:

- **Chapter 1 – History of and Introduction of Zero Trust**: This chapter provides the history of Zero Trust and analyses the driving forces such as

Ransomware attacks, digital modernization, the convergence of IT and operational technology, and so on. The chapter further explores the importance and the benefits of Zero Trust and attempted to introduce some of the most used standards, frameworks, and solution providers such as NIST ZT Framework, Forrester ZTX model, Gartner CARTA, Cloud Security Alliance SDP, Open Group, Netflix LISA model, Microsoft Zero Trust Model, and Google Beyond Corp approach. Finally, this chapter ends with an exciting perspective on how Zero trust resonates with everyone – government, enterprises, small businesses, and consumers.

- **Chapter 2 – Zero Trust – Disrupting the Business Model:** This chapter walks through the authors' perspectives on how Zero Trust disrupts the business model. It articulates why business leaders care about Zero Trust from an agility and cost reduction perspective. This chapter further explores the paradigm shift driven by the pandemic, the relevance of the organization culture for the successful adoption of Zero Trust. Finally, the chapter covers the human elements of ZTA by looking at the security leadership, security professionals, skills, and employees to determine the potential role in successful adoption.

- **Chapter 3 – Zero Trust Maturity and Implementation Assessment:** This chapter introduces our unique ZT Maturity Model created in partnership with Deakin University in Australia. We also share and introduce number of other maturity models by a few of the top industry vendors and organizations, such as Microsoft, Forrester, Palo Alto, and CISA, to choose from. These models are essential to help assess the readiness and build a plan to move to the next level of your Zero Trust journey.

- **Chapter 4 – Identity Is the New Security Control Plane:** Digital Identity Management is the heart and core of ZTA framework, we discuss how identity is a core part of an organization's security posture and plays a role in helping interconnect all other security solutions. We also share our perspective on the top four priorities in digital identity management.

- **Chapter 5 – Zero Trust Components:** In this chapter, we explore an implementation and architecture overview such as ZTA in a hybrid environment, ZT for identity architecture, ZT with SASE architecture, ZT for VPN replacement, and ZT for OT architecture. We also share many examples of architecture and real-life case studies.

- **Chapter 6 – Zero Trust Project Plan and Program Approach:** This is the last chapter of Part 2 of the book; this chapter provides an example of a project plan and a program approach. Readers can leverage this sample plan and customize it according to their organization's Zero Trust journey. The chapter outlines some of the lessons learned and mistakes to avoid during the Zero Trust journey.

- **Chapter 7 – Future Horizon of Zero Trust**: The chapter explores how Zero Trust will continue to evolve with AI; blockchain technology; the IoT; and governance, risk, and compliance capabilities.

Additional Resources

- Zero Trust Security Market Size Worth $59.43 Billion By 2028 | CAGR: 15.2%: Grand View Research, Inc. – Bloomberg

Part 1

History, Introduction, and Fundamentals of Zero Trust

Zero trust allows organizations to embrace the flexibility that their teams demand, while increasing the security of their systems. The question for security professionals isn't whether to embrace zero trust, the question is where are we along the journey?

Omkhar Arasaratnam, **Engineering Director, Google**

Chapter 1

History of and Introduction to Zero Trust

The adjective Zero Trust might be misleading at least to some of you. What does it mean? Does it mean "I don't trust you" or "there is no trust"? Before we explain what Zero Trust is, let us understand where it originated from history and how it become very popular in today's world.

The proverb rhymes in Russian – Doveryai, no proveryai – means that a responsible person always verifies everything before committing himself to a common business with anyone, even if that anyone is totally trustworthy.

In Russian, the saying turned into a much-overused cliché that can be used in all manner of circumstances, ranging from political negotiations to a spousal claim that a wife has a right to access her husband's smartphone anytime she likes because, well, doveryai, no proveryai (which basically implies that in both cases there's not much trust between the parties)!

"Doveryai, no proveryai" proverb simply popularized in the United States and internationally because President Reagan used it in American political discourse during the Cold War era. Reagan learned of the Russian proverb when he was preparing for talks with Soviet leader Mikhail Gorbachev. Reagan's adviser on Russia's affairs, Suzanne Massie, suggested the president to learn some Russian proverbs to amuse his counterpart. It turns out, Reagan liked "trust, but verify" the best. Later, Hillary Clinton, Barack Obama, and Colin Powell all used the English-translated phrase on multiple occasions – and attributed it to Ronald Reagan.

This proverb has been around for a long time. Russians have difficulty identifying its origins. The ultimate guide into Russian proverbs compiled and published by famous lexicographer Vladimir Dal in 1879 does not include this proverb. It means "trust but verify" and must have popped up only in the last years of the 19th or early 20th century.

Vladimir Lenin voiced a version of the idea (although not as elegantly) in his 1914 speech: "Do not take their word for it; check it strictly – this is the slogan of the Marxist workers!"

Joseph Stalin repeated Lenin's idea years later: "A healthy distrust is a good basis for working together".

DOI: 10.1201/9781003225096-3

1.1 Driving Forces

Cyberattacks continue to proliferate every year, and no sector seems to be immune. The rise in cyberattacks and ransomware has awakened business leaders all over the world to a new reality. The threats to network and data security have grown beyond what many traditional security solutions can defend against.

In recent times, we have seen supply chain attacks and breaches within our critical infrastructure. Government, large enterprises, and small businesses have experienced firsthand how sophisticated and well-financed criminal organizations, as well as nation-states, can wreak havoc by stealing sensitive data and disrupting operations.

Ransomware attacks take place 4,000 times worldwide every day. The process is reasonably straightforward – malware infects a target computer, and an attacker encrypts valuable data then sends the victim a notification demanding a ransom payment to release access to it. It's a gamble: even if the ransom is paid, there is no guarantee the attacker will release the data.

Digital modernization and the convergence of information technology (IT) and operational technology (OT) have greatly expanded the surface area of our networks and made them more vulnerable to attacks. Business leaders need to recognize the rapid growth in OT – which includes the Internet of Things (IoT), Industrial Internet of Things (IIoT), and industrial control system (ICS) – and understand that these devices and systems are on a converged IT– OT network using the same wires to transmit data. However, OT is not protected by traditional IT security solutions.

The typical IT-centric approach and tools currently used to protect communications fail to address known vulnerabilities inherent in the wide array of architectures, software, and equipment. This is because they are designed and built primarily for an "open" communications framework.

Given the number of vulnerable OT endpoints that are unprotected by IT security, cyber attackers have access to more endpoints they can exploit. Once inside a network, they can roam undetected for several months to a year, leaving malware and stealing data. And, nowadays, with the evolution of cloud computing, networks, and IT environments, the network perimeter security model is no longer sufficient.

1.2 What Is Zero Trust?

Zero Trust is a security framework requiring all users, whether in or outside the organization's network, to be authenticated, authorized, and continuously validated for security configuration and posture before being granted or keeping access to applications and data. Zero Trust assumes that there is no traditional network edge; networks can be local, in the cloud, or a combination or hybrid with resources anywhere as well as workers in any location (Figure 1.1).

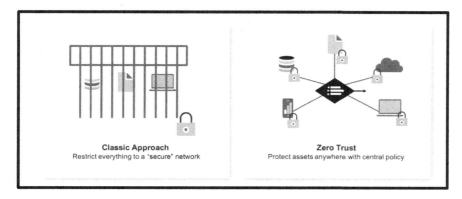

Figure 1.1 Classic Approach vs. Zero Trust.

1.3 The Inception of Zero Trust Concept

Zero Trust as a concept has been around for a while. This has been built upon over many years by various individuals and organization. This chapter introduces some of the most famous standards and frameworks that you can use to enhance your overall knowledge about this concept.

You can leverage any of these standards, frameworks, and principles based on your organization need, organization type, and your organization risk profile (Figure 1.2).

Looking back at history, in 2003, the Jericho Foundation introduced the concept of de-perimiterization. Later, in 2010, John Kindervag at Forrester wrote *Build Security Into Your Network's DNA: The Zero Trust Network Architecture*, and the term *Zero Trust* was born.

In 2013, Microsoft coined "Identity Driven Security" and introduced the Enterprise Mobility Suite (EMS) to address enterprises' core security and compliance needs – Secure Access, Secure Devices, and Secure Data.

That same year, Cloud Security Alliance's (CSA) Software-Defined Perimeter (SDP) concept. SDP was designed to create an invisible perimeter through a security architecture that requires positive identification of network connections from a single packet inspection before accessing resources.

In 2014, Google implemented a no-network trust model in "Beyond-Corp," providing a "demonstrator," which inspired tremendous interest. The approach revoled around the idea that the perimeter had expanded; hence traditional perimeter security and a protected intranet were no longer sufficient to protect against cyber threats.

In 2017, Gartner evolved their Adaptive Security Architecture to CARTA (Continuous Adaptive Risk and Trust Assessment). This improvement provided a framework to manage risk while taking advantage of the new digital world.

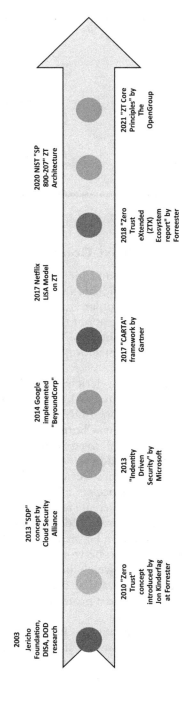

Figure 1.2 Zero Trust concept timeline.

That same year, Netflix introduced its Location Independent Security Assessment (LISA) model, which focuses more on the networking side of the architecture.

In 2018, Forrester analyst Dr. Chase Cunningham and his team published the Zero Trust eXtended (ZTX) Ecosystem report, which extends the original ZT model beyond its network focus to encompass today's ever-expanding attack surface.

In August 2020, National Institute of Standards and Technology (NIST) announced the final publication of Special Publication (SP) 800–207, Zero Trust architecture, which discusses the core logical components that make up Zero Trust architecture (ZTA).

In April 2021, The OpenGroup introduced a white paper on Zero Trust Core Principles that can be easily mapped with NIST 800–207 and Microsoft's Zero Trust Principles.

Let's look at some of the frameworks, standards, and its principles in detail.

1.3.1 Cloud Security Alliance's Software Define Perimeter and Zero Trust

CSA defines SDP as a network security architecture that is implemented to provide security at layers 1–7 of the Open Systems Interconnection (OSI) network stack. An SDP implementation hides assets and uses a single packet to establish trust via a separate control and data plane, before allowing connections to hidden assets.

> "Zero Trust is not SDP, but SDP is Zero Trust by definition"
>
> ~ CSA

SDP aims to give application owners the ability to deploy perimeter functionality where needed to isolate services from unsecured networks. SDP overlays existing physical infrastructure with logical components that should be operated under the control of the application owner. SDP provides access to application infrastructure only after device attestation and identity verification.

SDP is based on the construct that organizations should not implicitly trust anything inside or outside the network. It requires users on validated devices to cryptographically sign into the perimeter created to hide assets – even as they reside on public infrastructures. An SDP implementation hides assets with a deny-all firewall, uses a single packet to establish trust via a separate control plane, and provides mutual verification of connections in a data plane to hidden assets.

SDP integrates multiple controls typically fed into separate workstreams, such as applications, firewalls, and clients, and are hard to integrate. These pieces of information need to be pinned together to establish and ensure secure connections. SDP helps you to integrate controls for firewalls, identity credential and access management, encryption, and session and device management into a comprehensive security architecture that protects the application infrastructure from cyberattacks.

The SDP architecture is based upon the principles of least privilege and segregation of duties. These principles are enforced via the implementation of the following key concepts:

- dynamic rules on deny-all firewalls,
- hiding servers and services,
- authentication before connections, for example, not allowing connections before authorizing users on specific devices,
- using a single packet authorization (SPA) or bi-directional encrypted communications such as mutual Transport Layer Security (mTLS), and
- fine-grained access control and device validation.

1.3.2 Google's BeyondCorp Zero Trust Model

The BeyondCorp Enterprise solution delivers three benefits to customers and partners.

"A scalable, reliable zero-trust platform in a secure, agentless architecture, including continuous and real-time end-to-end protection and provides a solution that's open and extensible, to support a wide variety of complementary solutions."

~ Google

BeyondCorp is Google's implementation of the Zero Trust model. It builds upon a decade of experience at Google, combined with ideas and best practices from the community. By shifting access controls from the network perimeter to individual users, BeyondCorp enables secure work from virtually any location without the need for a traditional VPN (Figure 1.3). The two most important tenets of BeyondCorp are:

Controlling access to the network and applications: In BeyondCorp, all decisions about giving a person or device access to a network are made through an access control engine. This engine sits in front of every network request and applies rules and access policies based on

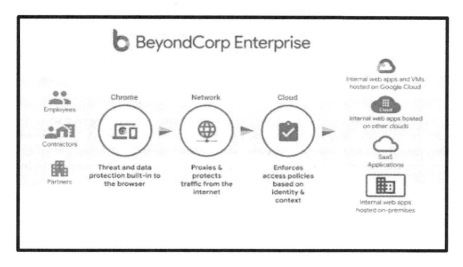

Figure 1.3 BeyondCorp Enterprise Implementation Model.
Image Source *https://cloud.google.com/beyondcorp-enterprise*

the context of each request – such as user identity, device information, and location – and the amount of sensitive data in an application. It provides organizations with an automated, scalable way to
verify a user's identity, confirms they're authorized, and apply rules
and access policies. However, access control alone is not enough to
ensure adequate security.

Visibility: Once a user has access to an organization's network or applications, the organization must continually view and inspect all traffic
to identify any unauthorized activity or malicious content. Otherwise,
an attacker can easily move around within the network and take
whatever data they want without anyone knowing.

Similar to other Zero Trust approach as discussed, BeyondCrop also removes
the implicit trust approach and requires user verification using various components such as identity, device, and cloud services by following the below
set of principles:

- Enable users to securely access all resources, regardless of location.
- Use a least-privilege strategy and strictly enforce access control.
- Inspect and log all traffic.

1.3.3 Gartner's CARTA Framework for Zero Trust

www.ssh.com/academy/iam/carta

"Zero trust is a security paradigm that replaces implicit trust with continuously assessed explicit risk/trust levels based on context – most notably identity – that adapts to risk-optimize the organization's security posture.

~ Gartner"

Gartner introduced CARTA in 2010 as an evolution of adaptive security architecture and strategic approach to IT security that favors continuous cybersecurity assessments and contextual decision-making based on adaptive evaluations of risk and trust. CARTA also follows the same philosophy of moving from Block and Allow to a fuzzier form of provisioning access at a certain level depending on trust level and confidence and risk level.

Companies that offer digital services to consumers must, by nature, open up aspects of their corporate network to many more users than they ever would have in the past. With the rapid growth and development of cloud services and bring your own device (BYOD), especially since the recent COVID pandemic, and accepting the fact that users may work from anywhere other than corporate network, organizations need to be more flexible in accommodating unmanaged devices and applications in an organization's operation model and workplace.

CARTA uses risk based and contextual decision making. It does not widely open every asset accessible to all, but it grants access more granularly with higher transparency regardless of where the authorized user is located (Figure 1.4).

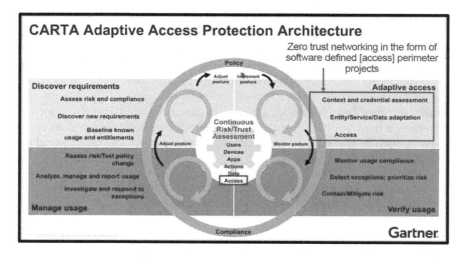

Figure 1.4 CARTA Adaptive Access Protection Architecture.

1.3.3.1 CARTA's Zero Trust Implementation Approach

CARTA advises continuously evaluating all users or devices and making contextual access decisions. It's rooted in the Zero Trust framework, which advocates that no user or device – even those that are already within the network – should be inherently trusted.

The three phases of CARTA IT security and risk management

Run: In this phase, organizations rely on analytics to detect anomalies in real time. Automated solutions allow this detection to happen regularly and much sooner than if this evaluation were done manually. The net benefit is that the organization can respond to potential threats much sooner.

Build: This phase goes hand in hand with the concept of DevSecOps. It involves baking security into the development process by always evaluating and identifying security risks before they are built into production code. Since many modern applications are pieced together using publicly available libraries mixed with custom code, organizations need to make sure they are scanning these libraries for security risks before adding it to their program. Similarly, companies must evaluate ecosystem partners, including third-party developers and digital service providers, who need to interact with their environment.

Planning: Finally, organizations need to set their priorities. How much security risk are business leaders willing to accept in order to tap into the new opportunities afforded by modern IT environments? If your organization decides it wants to move to the public cloud, how will you address the security implications inherent in that decision? If remote work is preferred among your staff, how will the IT environment need to evolve in order to support that? By thinking through modern IT and establishing priorities, businesses will be in a better position to make contextual decisions and avoid the black–white decision-making processes of traditional IT.

CARTA implementation makes the most sense for enterprises and organizations with:

- Large numbers of agentless internet of things devices
- An extensive network of external vendors or partners requiring network access
- An active BYOD policy
- A large remote workforce
- A growing network perimeter
- Issues arising from silos within existing security systems
- Concerns regarding the use of unapproved third-party applications

Such complex networks have more users, including third parties, and require more oversight and automation than smaller network environments. Customer access introduces additional challenges for some enterprises and organizations. CARTA can also address these issues, such as unsecure devices and access from private Wi-Fi connections.

If a breach occurs, the CARTA model improves detection times and allows for faster responses. Instead of weeks or months passing between a breach event and its discovery, enterprises can shut down and mitigate hacker activity before extensive damage is done.

1.3.4 Netflix's LISA Model for Zero Trust

Netflix developed LISA as an inter-organizational framework by simplifying the primary focus to their business nature and wide global user reach. They focus more on the user identity and health regardless of the user location. Looking at the LISA model, you can find similarities with Google BeyondCorp model to some extent. Organizations that promote work from home (WFH) or anywhere, even during your Caribbean beach holiday, could leverage this model as long as the user is authenticated rightfully, and the device meets the required security controls and compliance level.

> "LISA Model is all about: Trust identity and health, not location."
> ~ Abbas Kudrati

1.3.4.1 LISA Principles

The LISA model operates on three core principles.

1   Trust identity and health.
2   No trust in the office network.
3   Device isolation.

The benefit of the LISA model is that it reduces the attack surface by stopping attacks such as "man in the middle" (MITM) attacks. It acts as a choke point for authentication, access, and inspection. And it also helps you check endpoint security posture.

It further helps in simplifying the network architecture. The same solution is used inside and outside the office with little or no custom development. And it is not tied to a set of supported vendors.

The LISA model manages endpoints by promoting manage your own device (MYOD) and health checks instead of central management. Netflix has created its own custom code for user identity and device security verification, its "Stethoscope and Trainman."

Within their offices, end users get an internet connection and VPN services; no other services are provided when working in the office.

Google's BeyondCorp model influences the LISA model; the main differentiator of the LISA model versus Google Beyond is that BeyondCrop uses proxy in front of the applications instead of VPN, while LISA uses VPN and without a proxy service. The LISA model has similar principles but a minor feature set as compared with Google's model.

1.3.5 Forrester's ZTX Framework

Zero Trust has turned more than 10 years old now. John Kindervag's research and analysis of enterprises uncovered those dangerous assumptions of "trust" had become an essential part of the network. He realized that the human emotion of trust was more than a simple flaw; it represented a major liability for enterprises' networks that would lead to failure over and over again in the years to come.

Since 2010, attackers have breached thousands of companies, stealing billions of records. Some companies went out of business, some governments suffered geopolitical setbacks that would take years to unravel, and many citizens have lost faith in the integrity of their countries' electoral procedures. And none of those exploits or breaches ever required attackers to use their most sophisticated skills or techniques. Most of them began with the failure of a few basic security controls and the inevitable lateral movement of attackers.

Zero Trust wasn't born out of a need to sell another security control or solution. It was born from a desire to solve a real enterprise issue. And just as the threat landscape and the challenges have evolved over the past 10 years, Forrester has worked to build out the original concept into a simple framework called ZTX.

The ZTX framework solves the architectural and operational issues with Zero Trust – namely, how to get started and how to sustain a Zero Trust approach. ZTX covers how to "build" Zero Trust into the technology stack of your enterprise. It helps organizations understand how they can choose solutions that deliver on Zero Trust principles that enable their strategy over time.

Trust is the fundamental problem in information security today. If the current trust model is broken, how do we fix it? It requires a new way of thinking. The way we fix the old trust model is to look for a new trust model. Forrester calls this new model "Zero Trust". The Zero Trust Model is simple: security professionals must stop trusting packets as if they were people. Instead, they must eliminate the idea of a trusted network (usually the internal network) and an untrusted network (external networks). In Zero Trust, all network traffic is untrusted. Thus, security professionals (1) must verify and secure all resources, (2) limit and strictly enforce access control, and (3) inspect and log all network traffic. These are three fundamental concepts of the Forrester Zero Trust Model. By changing our trust model, we can change our networks and make them easier to build and maintain; we can even make them more efficient, more compliant, and more cost-effective. By changing the trust model, we reduce the temptation for insiders to abuse or misuse the network, and we improve our chances of discovering cybercrime before it can succeed.

In the Zero Trust Model, security professionals must:

- **Ensure all resources are accessed securely regardless of location**: When you eliminate the concept of trust from the network, it becomes natural to ensure that all resources are securely accessed – no matter who creates the traffic or from where it originates.
- **Assume that all traffic is threat traffic until determined otherwise . . .** You must make this assumption until you can verify that the traffic is authorized, inspected, and secured. In real-world situations, this often necessitates using encrypted tunnels for accessing data on both internal and external networks. Cybercriminals can easily sniff unencrypted data; thus, Zero Trust demands that security professionals protect internal data from insider abuse in the same manner as they protect external data on the public internet.
- **. . . regardless of location or hosting model.** This is especially important as we move to a cloud-enabled technology environment where much of the data sits outside of our traditional data centers. Also, Zero Trust is helpful in enforcing data-residency issues related to the new data privacy regulations emerging around the globe. Zero Trust networks are data-centric and have powerful embedded data control mechanisms
- **Adopt a least privileged strategy and strictly enforce access control**: When we properly implement and enforce access control, by default we help eliminate the human temptation to access restricted resources. For example, in 2013, prestigious Los Angeles hospital Cedars-Sinai fired six employees after they accessed the protected health information of 14 patients, which included one high-profile celebrity. Not only can strict access control help protect against malicious attacks, but it will also keep embarrassing and possibly even life-threatening incidents from happening.
- **Provide role-based access controls for all employees**: Today, role-based access control (RBAC) is a standard technology supported by network access control and infrastructure software, identity and access management systems, and many applications. With RBAC, security professionals place users into a role and based upon that role they are allowed access to certain specific resources. Zero Trust does not explicitly define RBAC as the preferred access control methodology. Other technologies and methodologies will evolve over time. What's important is the concept of minimal privileges and strict access control. It's also important

that the security pros have an appropriate identity and access governance strategy in place to periodically review and recertify employees' access rights.

- **Implement Privileged Identity Management (PIM) for access to sensitive systems**: Employees who have administrative access to sensitive applications and systems can wreak havoc for a firm if they have malicious intent. They can delete sensitive data or even entire systems and they can download sensitive data. They are also often the target of hackers hoping to compromise their credentials for their own ends. PIM solutions allow security pros to closely monitor the activities of these users and require them to check out passwords to gain access to sensitive systems.
- **Inspect and log all traffic**: In Zero Trust, someone will assert their identity, and then we will allow them access to a particular resource based upon that assertion. We will restrict users only to the resources they need to perform their jobs.

But Zero Trust does not stop there; it requires security and risk professionals to:

- **Continuously inspect user traffic for signs of suspicious activity**: Instead of trusting users to do the right thing, we verify that they are doing the right thing. To do this, we simply flip the mantra "trust but verify" into "verify and never trust". By continuously inspecting network traffic, security pros can identify anomalous user behavior or suspicious user activity (e.g., a user performing large downloads or frequently accessing systems or records he normally doesn't need to for his day-to-day responsibilities).
- **Continuously log and analyze all network traffic**: Zero Trust advocates two methods of gaining network traffic visibility: inspection and logging. Many security professionals do log internal network traffic, but this approach is passive and doesn't provide the real-time protection capabilities necessary in this new threat environment. Zero Trust promotes the idea that you must inspect traffic as well as log it. Based on our experiences and evidenced by such data breaches as Heartland Payment Systems, the U.S. Military Central Command attack, and even the 2013 Target attack, Forrester believes that there is very little inspection of internal network traffic. Zero Trust network topology makes it easier to send traffic and logs to security analytics tools for deeper analysis.

Source: https://go.forrester.com/blogs/tag/ztx/

1.3.6 NIST SP 800:207 Zero Trust Framework

> "Zero trust (ZT) provides a collection of concepts and ideas designed to minimize uncertainty in enforcing accurate, least privilege per-request access decisions in information systems and services in the face of a network viewed as compromised. Zero Trust architecture (ZTA) is an enterprise's cybersecurity plan that utilizes zero trust concepts and encompasses component relationships, workflow planning, and access policies".
>
> – National Institute of Standards and Technology (NIST), U.S. Department of Commerce

1.3.6.1 NIST's Zero Trust Architecture Foundation

Organizations need to note that Zero Trust is not a plug-and-play sort of appliance or software to be installed within the organization network and make the magic. It requires business, IT, and security cultural changes and certain maturity levels, as discussed in Chapters 2 and 3 of this book.

The Zero Trust architecture put forward by NIST is a detailed guide for enterprises and organizations to begin their Zero Trust journey. However, there is no one perfect method to implement Zero Trust architecture. To some extent, you could modify existing identity and access management tools to follow Zero Trust principles, but adopting the right security tools can make your Zero Trust journey simpler and efficient. A good start would be to look for solutions that provide real-time visibility of all network communications. Once you fully understand your network, investing in a robust policy engine that can enforce policies across dynamic network environments can implement Zero Trust possible without increasing complexity.

Before implementing NIST-based Zero Trust architecture, several foundation elements need to be defined and deployed in place as brief as follows:

1   **Defining devices:** To implement Zero Trust effectively, the enterprise needs to consider all data sources and computing services as resources. These may include devices that share data with aggregators, software as a service (SaaS), and different types of endpoints that connect and communicate with the network.
2   **Securing communications:** All access requests from assets must meet present security requirements. The assets may be located on enterprise-owned network infrastructure or any external network – the same security verifications must be applicable to all. Trust can never be implicit.
3   **Session-based resource access:** Trust must be established before authorizing access to any enterprise resource, and the trust must be applicable

only for the duration of the transaction. Authorization of access to a specific resource cannot be extended to access a different resource.

4 **Attribute-based policy enforcement:** Policy is the set of access rules based on attributes that an organization assigns to a user, data asset, or application. These attributes could be device characteristics such as software version, location, time of request, and so on. Behavioral attributes defined by user and device analytics may also be considered based on sensitivity of the resource.

5 **Dynamic authentication and authorization:** Granting access, scanning and assessing threats, and continually reevaluating trust must be an ongoing process. Asset management systems and multi-factor authentication (MFA) need to be in place along with continuous monitoring to ensure that re-authentication and reauthorization are based on defined policies.

6 **Policy fine-tuning:** Enterprises must collect as much information as possible about the current state of the network and communications, using this data to continually improve their security posture. Insights provided by this data help to create new policies where needed and fine-tune existing security policies to enforce proactive protection (Figure 1.5).

According to NIST, implementing Zero Trust requires an architecture or framework with specific logical components. This architecture should monitor the flow of data into and within the network and control access to resources to ensure that trust is never implicit.

As such, verification is at the center of the Zero Trust architecture. Any and all access requests should be verified according to defined security policies before authorization. Considering how complex enterprise networks are, implementation of Zero Trust can be simplified by deploying solutions that allow context-based, dynamic policy enforcement across data center and hybrid cloud environments.

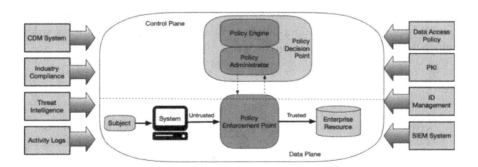

Figure 1.5 Core Zero Trust logical components.

This can be achieved when the architecture has the following core components in place:

- A policy engine
- A policy administrator
- A policy enforcement point

1.3.6.2 Policy Engine

The policy engine is the core of Zero Trust architecture. The policy engine relies on policies orchestrated by the enterprise's security team and data from external sources such as security information and event management (SIEM) or threat intelligence to verify and determine context. The policy engine decides whether to grant access to any resource within the network. Access is then granted, denied, or revoked based on the parameters defined by the enterprise. The policy engine communicates with a policy administrator component that executes the decision.

1.3.6.3 Policy Administrator

The policy administrator component is responsible for executing access decisions determined by the policy engine. It has the ability to allow or deny the communication path between a subject and a resource. Once the policy engine makes an access decision, the policy administrator kicks in to allow or deny a session by communicating a third logical component called the policy enforcement point.

1.3.6.4 Policy Enforcement Point

The policy enforcement point is responsible for enabling, monitoring, and terminating connections between a subject and an enterprise resource. In theory, this is treated as a single component of Zero Trust architecture. But in practice, the policy enforcement point has two sides: 1) the client side, which could be an agent on a laptop or a server; and 2) the resource side, which acts as a gateway to control access.

1.3.7 The Open Group Zero Trust's Approach

> Zero Trust brings security to the users, data/information, applications, APIs, devices, networks, cloud, etc. wherever they are – instead of forcing them onto a "secure" network. In other words, Zero Trust shifts the perceived role of security restricting business to security enabling business.
>
> ~ *www.opengroup.org*

The Open Group ZTA Working Group defines Zero Trust as "an information security approach that focuses on data/information security, including lifecycle, on any platform or network" and Zero Trust architecture as "the implementation of a Zero Trust security strategy that follows well-defined and assured standards, technical patterns, and guidance for organizations".

The Open Group ZTA Working Group believes that Zero Trust reduces the impact area, or blast radius, of a breach in addition to minimizing the threat space that needs to be protected against. Zero Trust enables organizational agility and the ability to operate in a situation of assumed breach.

1.3.7.1 Key Requirements for Zero Trust as per the Open Group

The key drivers already discussed help define the requirements to determine the capabilities that a Zero Trust must support. As shown in Figure 1.6, these requirements tend to disrupt existing processes and models, defining capabilities that a modern information security architecture must support for the Digital Age (Figure 1.7).

Here is a quick summary of the Open Group Zero Trust principles from the source website.

1.3.7.2 Organizational Value and Risk Alignment

1   **Modern work enablement** – Users in organizational ecosystems must be able to work on any network in any location with the same security assurances, increasing productivity.
2   **Goal alignment** – Security must align with and enable organization goals within risk tolerance and threshold.
3   **Risk alignment** – Security risk must be managed and measured consistently using the organization's risk framework and considering organizational risk tolerance and thresholds.

1.3.7.3 Guardrails and Governance

4   **People guidance and inspiration** – Organizational governance frameworks must guide people, process, and technology decisions with clear ownership of decisions, policy, and aspirational visions.
5   **Risk and complexity reduction** – Governance must both reduce complexity (i.e., simplify) and reduce threat surface area.
6   **Alignment and automation** – Policies and security success metrics must map directly to organizational mission and risk requirements and should favor automated execution and reporting.
7   **Security for the full lifecycle** – Risk analysis and confidentiality, integrity, and availability assurances must be sustained for the lifetime of the data,

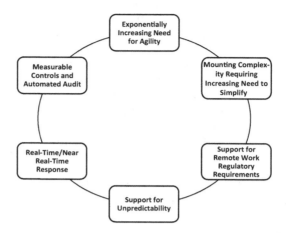

Figure 1.6 ZT requirements.

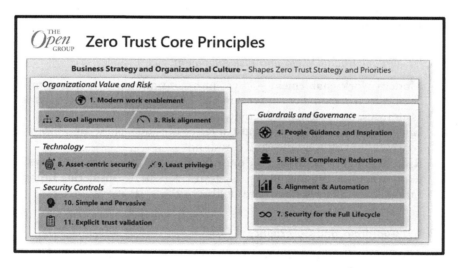

Figure 1.7 The Open Group's Zero Trust core principles.

Source: www.opengroup.org/forum/security/zerotrust

transaction, or relationship. Asset sensitivity must be reduced where possible (e.g., removing sensitive/regulated data, privileges), and assurances should be provided for the risk of data in use, in-flight, and at rest.

1.3.7.4 Technology

8   **Asset-centric security** – Security must be as close to the assets as possible (e.g., data-centric and application-centric approaches instead of network-centric strategies) to provide a tailored approach that minimizes productivity disruption.
9   **Least privilege** – Access to systems and data must be granted only as required and removed when no longer required.

1.3.7.5 Security Controls

10   **Simple and pervasive** – Security mechanisms must be simple, scalable, and easy to implement and manage throughout the organizational ecosystem (whether internal or external).
11   **Explicit trust validation** – Assumptions of integrity and trust level must be explicitly validated against organization risk threshold and tolerance. Assets and data systems must be validated before being allowed to interact with anyone or anything else.

1.3.8 Microsoft's Zero Trust Principles

Microsoft distilled Zero Trust tenets into three principles: verify explicitly, use least privileged access, and assume breach. Microsoft uses these principles for our strategic guidance to customers, software development, and global security posture.

- **Verify explicitly** – Always authenticate and authorize based on all available data points, including user identity, location, device health, service or workload, data classification, and anomalies.
- **Use least privileged access** – Limit user access with just-in-time and just-enough-access (JIT/JEA), risk-based adaptive policies, and data protection to help secure both data and productivity.
- **Assume breach** – Minimize blast radius and segment access. Verify end-to-end encryption and use analytics to get visibility, drive threat detection, and improve defenses (Figure 1.8).

1.4 Why Zero Trust Is Important

Zero Trust is one of the most effective ways for organizations to control access to their networks, applications, and data. It combines a wide range of preventative techniques, including identity verification and behavioral analysis, micro-segmentation, data, endpoint security, least privilege controls, and understanding of the data criticality and sensitivity to deter would-be attackers and limit their access in the event of a breach.

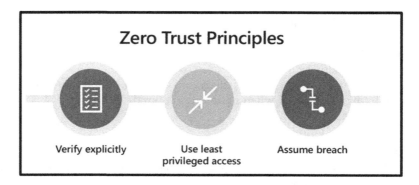

Figure 1.8 Microsoft's Zero Trust Principles.
Source: http://aka.ms/zerotrust

It is not enough to establish firewall rules and block by packet analysis – a compromised account that passes authentication protocols at a network perimeter device should still be evaluated for each subsequent session or endpoint it attempts to access. Having the technology to recognize normal versus abnormal behavior allows organizations to step up authentication controls and policies rather than assume connection via VPN or Secure Web Gateway means the connection is fully safe and trusted.

This added layer of security is critical as companies increase the number of endpoints within their network and expand their infrastructure to include cloud-based applications and servers – not to mention the explosion of service accounts on microsites and other machines hosted locally, Virtual Machine (VM), or via SaaS. These trends make it more challenging to establish, monitor, and maintain secure perimeters. Furthermore, a borderless security strategy is vital for organizations with a global workforce that offer employees the ability to work remotely.

Finally, by segmenting the network by identity, groups, and function and controlling user access, Zero Trust security helps the organization contain breaches and minimize potential damage. This is an important security measure as rogue credentials (insider or compromised) orchestrate some of the most sophisticated attacks.

1.5 Benefits of Zero Trust

The core purpose of Zero Trust is to understand and control how users, processes, and devices access the network, data, and resources. The combination of the user, device, and any other security-relevant contextual information (e.g., location, time of day, previous logged behavior of the user or device) is used to grant access.

All requests are authenticated (verified) before access is granted to the data, network, or resources. The result of implementing a ZTA is the gain of a controlled environment.

By simplifying and standardizing the approach, ZTA can become an enabler for business and new business opportunities.

Some of ZTA's benefits for an organization are:

1   Improved cybersecurity and reduced risk of compromise

- Reduce attack surface and its impact
- Increase attacker's cost by reducing an attacker's ability to move laterally
- Improve Mean Time to Acknowledge and Mean time to Detect

2   Strong identity and increased focus on trusted access

- Strong authentication, password security (passwordless and MFA)
- Granular access and permissions for device and network access as well as for users and resource access.
- Enforce least privilege, centralized access control
- Improved user experience and workforce flexibility
- Continuous validation of identity, authentication, and authorization to resources
- Context based access control
- Role- and behavior-based data protection

3   Improved security monitoring and analytics

- Advance logging and monitoring offer greater visibility across the enterprise
- Monitoring analytics over user (entities) behavior
- Network isolation and micro-segmentation improve the ability to detect and quickly isolate the impact of an attack.
- Micro-segmentation facilitates access control to each resource via fine-grained authorization
- Continuous monitoring across all attack surfaces makes it easier to detect data breaches and enforce appropriate responses
- Improves resource protection with JIT and JEA

4   Improved compliance management

- Continuous user (entities) behavior monitoring support continuous auditing and continuous compliance
- Micro-segmentation and enforcement of the least privilege reduce the regulatory compliance scope while supporting compliance objectives

5   Simplification, cost benefits, and other potential benefits

- Cost reduction
- Simplification of IT management design   '
- Improved data protection for business-critical data and customer data
- Secure remote access
- Continuous and progressively greater compliance

1.6 Zero Trust Principle Redefined

You see similarities in principles from NIST, Open Group, Forrester, and Microsoft. We want to provide additional principles that organizations of all sizes can consider and adopt. It is not necessary to apply all principles to every organization. Based on your needs and organizational maturity, you can choose the right principle to develop a Zero Trust plan.

Instead of assuming everything behind the corporate firewall is safe, the Zero Trust model assumes breach and verifies each request as though it originates from an open network. Regardless of where the request originates or what resource it accesses, Zero Trust teaches us to "never trust, always verify". Every access request is fully authenticated, authorized, and encrypted before granting access. Micro-segmentation and least privileged access principles are applied to minimize lateral movement. Rich intelligence and analytics are utilized to detect and respond to anomalies in real time.

The following principles come with additional perspectives that can be relevant for organizations of all sizes.

- Re-examine all default access controls
- Micro-segmentation
- Preventing lateral movement
- Leveraging a variety of preventive techniques
- Enable real-time monitoring and controls to identify and halt malicious activity
- Align to a broader security strategy

1.6.1 Re-Examine All Default Access Controls

In a Zero Trust model, **there is no such thing as a trusted source**. The model assumes would-be attackers are present both inside and outside the network. As such, every request to access the system must be authenticated, authorized, and encrypted.

1.6.2 Micro-Segmentation

Zero Trust networks also utilize micro-segmentation. Micro-segmentation is breaking up security perimeters into small zones to maintain separate access for separate parts of the network. For example, a network with files living in a single data center that utilizes micro-segmentation may contain dozens of separate, secure zones. A person or program with access to one of these zones will not be able to access any of the other zones without separate authorization.

1.6.3 Preventing Lateral Movement

In network security, "lateral movement" is when an attacker moves within a network after gaining access to that network. Lateral movement can be difficult to detect even if the attacker's entry point is discovered because the attacker will have gone on to compromise other parts of the network. The attack surface in minimized as ZTA only allows access at the application level, not at the network level, thus the intellectual property (IP) stack is somewhat protected, and the underlying vulnerabilities that may reside on the infrastructure are not accessible.

Zero Trust is designed to contain attackers so that they cannot move laterally. Because Zero Trust access is segmented and must be re-established periodically, an attacker cannot move across to other micro-segments within the network. Once the attacker's presence is detected, the compromised device or user account can be quarantined, cut off from further access. (In a castle-and-moat model, if lateral movement is possible for the attacker, quarantining the original compromised device or user has little to no effect, since the attacker will already have reached other parts of the network.)

1.6.4 Leverage a Variety of Preventative Techniques

A Zero Trust model relies on a variety of preventative techniques to stop breaches and minimize their damage:

- **Identity protection and device discovery** are core to a Zero Trust model. Keeping credentials and devices in an audit-ready state of knowing what devices exist and which credentials are on each is the first step in Zero Trust, establishing what is normal and expected on the extended network ecosystem. Knowing how these devices and credentials behave and connect allows organizations to employ effective identity challenges and step-up authentication for anomalies.
- Multi Factor Authentication (MFA) is one of the most common ways to confirm the user's identity and increase the security of the network. MFA relies on two or more pieces of evidence, including security questions, email or text confirmation, or logic-based exercises to assess the user's credibility. The number of authentication factors an organization uses is directly proportional to network security – meaning that incorporating more authentication points will help strengthen the organization's overall security.

Zero Trust also prevents attacks through **least-privilege access**, which means that the organization grants the lowest level of access possible to each user or device. In the event of a breach, this helps limit lateral movement across the network and minimizes the attack surface.

1.6.5 Enable Real-Time Monitoring and Controls to Identify and Halt Malicious Activity Quickly

While a Zero Trust model is largely preventative in nature, the organization should also incorporate real-time monitoring capabilities to improve their "breakout time" – the critical window between when an intruder compromises the first machine and when they can move laterally to other systems on the network. Real-time monitoring is essential to the organization's ability to detect, investigate, and remediate intrusions.

Identity challenges need to occur in real time as they happen at the domain controller rather than merely logged and passed to a SIEM. Brute force attacks against credentials and suspicious movement to critical systems like the domain controller need to be stopped or challenged as they occur and then sent to monitoring systems to collate against other incursions and attempts.

1.6.6 Align to the Broader Security Strategy

A Zero Trust architecture is just one aspect of a comprehensive security strategy. In addition, while technology plays an important part in protecting the organization, digital capabilities alone will not prevent breaches. Companies must adopt a holistic security solution that incorporates a variety of endpoint monitoring, detection, and response capabilities to ensure the safety of their networks.

Companies should examine (and update) older or obsolete authentication protocols like LDAP and NTLM wherever possible, removing "easy access" for identity attacks. And consistent with security advice since the dawn of time, all devices, services, applications, and firmware should be patched as quickly as possible when new zero-day vulnerabilities are announced by vendors.

Finally, as we learned from the recent Sunburst attacks, even innocent-seeming software updates to common systems can potentially cause damage. Having a solid incident response plan as well as business continuity and recovery plans helps at both ends of any unexpected incidents or potential breaches.

1.7 Zero Trust for Everyone

The concept behind the increasingly popular Zero Trust security strategy is simple: trust no one. Taking it one level deeper, Zero Trust helps every organization and institution to implement, enforce, and maintain strict access controls by adopting an approach to security in which IT and security teams do not trust anyone or any action by default – even if a user is already inside the network perimeter. When it comes to network access, zero trust starts with a default deny posture for everyone – government, enterprises, small businesses, and consumers.

Instead, users must authenticate themselves before they are granted further access to systems, IP addresses, machines, and so on, and each individual transaction is evaluated based on need and risk. The biggest benefits of Zero Trust in the corporate world are stronger access control and minimized risk associated with overly permissive, unnecessary, or outdated user privileges.

1.7.1 Government

President Joe Biden's cybersecurity executive order, signed May 12, 2021, calls for the federal government to adopt a ZTA. This raises a couple of questions. What if trust is bad for cybersecurity? And why do most organizations in government and the private sector do it?

There were at least 2,354 ransomware attacks on local governments, health care facilities, and schools in the United States in 2020. Although estimates vary, losses to ransomware seem to have tripled in 2020 to more than US$300,000 per incident. And ransomware attacks are growing more sophisticated.

As federal agencies continue to support large numbers of remote workers, IT leaders have started to evolve their thinking on Zero Trust security architectures. Increasingly, they are becoming more comfortable with the concept and are seeking to lay the foundation for deployments.

Zero trust represents a mindset shift in cybersecurity in which every transaction is verified before access is granted to users and devices. In the federal government, it is still a relatively nascent approach, with some pilot programs here and there. However, IT leaders seem to recognize that cybersecurity models are increasingly going to be defined by a Zero Trust architecture.

In the United States, the Defense Department, the Department of Education, and the Small Business Administration are among the agencies that are warming to Zero Trust and see it on their roadmaps.

1.7.2 Enterprises

There are plenty of valid business reasons for enterprises to adopt the Zero Trust model now and in the foreseeable future.

- **Perimeter-based security is ineffective in the evolving enterprise**: The way enterprises conduct business and use digital technologies is evolving constantly – and at an ever-quickening pace. These digital transformations are making traditional perimeter-based cybersecurity models ineffective and irrelevant because perimeters no longer define the scope of security enforcement.

  Only Zero Trust security takes a micro-level approach to authenticating and approving access requests at every point within a network. The concept of least privilege means that nobody gets unrestricted access to the entire system. Instead, each request needs to be continuously monitored and verified to gain access to different parts of the network. If a breach does occur, micro-segmentation will prevent lateral movement and minimize the damage that could be caused by a threat actor.

- **Cloud data centers require shared security responsibility**: Critical applications and workloads are moving from corporate-owned data centers to the public or hybrid cloud. Now, security leaders need to reconsider the legacy assumptions of trust around people and data center security tools, technologies, processes, and skills.

  This new cloud environment requires a shared responsibility model, in which certain security aspects are provided by the cloud vendor and others fall on the enterprise. The underlying assumption of trust in the infrastructure is no longer the same. A Zero Trust model can span this shared cybersecurity responsibility.

- **The internet network is an unsecured network**: Applications and workloads have moved to the cloud, and users access them remotely. This means that the network is no longer a secured enterprise network. Instead, it is an unsecured internet. The network perimeter security and visibility solutions employed by most businesses to keep attackers out are no longer practical or robust enough. The concept of implicit trust is no longer effective.

  Zero trust employs least-privilege and "always-verify" principles, offering complete visibility within the network, whether in data centers or the cloud.

- **Everyone in the expanding workforce shouldn't have all access**: The way enterprises conduct their critical business and the people they rely on to perform key functions have changed. Network users are no longer just employees and customers. Many users who access a business's applications and infrastructure could be vendors servicing a system, suppliers, or partners.

  None of these non-employees need, or should have, access to all applications, infrastructure, or business data. Even employees perform specialized functions and therefore do not need complete network access. A well-executed Zero Trust strategy allows authenticated access based on key dimensions of trust. This enables businesses to control access more precisely, even to those with elevated privileges.

- **You cannot verify the security status of all work from home (WFH) environments**: In the pre-COVID era, remote work was not uncommon. However, now that WFH has become the new normal after the pandemic, security technologies and processes based purely on established geographic locations – such as a company's headquarters – are no longer relevant. With a remote workforce, the possibility of unsecured Wi-Fi networks and devices increases security risks exponentially.

Enterprises must assume their employees' WFH setups and environ-ments are not as secure as the office. Their Wi-Fi router isn't config-ured for WPA-2. Their IoT devices, such as the baby monitor or the smart thermostat, are running a hodge-podge of security protocols, if any at all. Without an overarching system like a Zero Trust framework, whether or not employees are working in a secure environment can no longer be verified – or controlled.

- **BYOD is not as secure as work devices**: Under the WFH new nor-mal, the devices that workers use are less likely to be ones assigned by the employer. Employer-owned laptops and phones are traditionally managed, patched, and kept up to date with security tools and policies. However, with everyone working remotely, employees may forget the basic cyber hygiene skills and start to use their own devices to access work networks or apps. Or they could be using their work laptops to shop online between Zoom calls.

  Even if Zero Trust security can't force employees working at home to use work devices only for work, it can control the potential for a security breach because of the fundamental "trust nobody; verify everything" rule that enforces access controls at every point within the network.

- **Cyberattacks are increasing**: Cyberattacks continue to proliferate every year, and no sector seems to be immune. During COVID-19, hackers focused on the health care and retail verticals for pandemic-related reasons. Overburdened hospitals struggling with an onslaught of patients and pharmaceutical research labs racing to develop a vaccine have been ideal targets for cyberattacks. The stakes are so high that they are willing to pay vast ransoms to ensure business continuity. Cybercriminals have targeted online retailers benefiting from increased e-commerce demands during shelter in place. They've also attacked financial institutions and even transportation service providers.

  With Zero Trust architecture in place, these businesses could build a better security posture and become cyber resilient. Then they will be less vulnerable to security breaches and would be better equipped to contain and mitigate financial or reputational damage.

- **The security stakes are higher**: Instead of deploying distributed denial of service (DDoS) attacks to disrupt businesses, cybercriminals are starting to play an almost elegant long game. Cyberattacks have evolved to tar-get user data, customer data, financial data, and core business knowl-edge, such as IP and proprietary functions – essentially anything that could be valuable. Core government systems, weapons, nuclear power plants, and even elections are at risk. Because the stakes are so high, at every level of society and government, robust and resilient cybersecurity strategies are of paramount importance.

Whether implemented by a multinational enterprise or a government agency, the Zero Trust framework will improve cybersecurity posture and increase cyber resilience, enabling containment in the unlikely event of a breach.

In summary, the perimeter-based, reactive methods that acted as the foundation of old, traditional security need to become relics of the past. Enterprises must be proactive and adopt Zero Trust now to confidently provide a cyber-secure future to their customers, partners, and employees.

It's time to make security a priority to protect, detect, and mitigate modern-day threats. Only this new-gen Zero Trust security framework offers network visibility and constant monitoring that allows trust to be dynamic and context-based, by verifying every access request and authorizing access only if certain parameters are met.

1.7.3 Small and Medium Businesses

Most successful small businesses and growing startups share the common trait of moving at a quick pace. They're hiring new employees and contractors and adding new locations in days, not months. Each new employee, contractor, and occasional supplier receives their account login to cloud systems used for running the business, and then they're given their first assignments.

Small businesses and startups run so fast there's often a perception that achieving greater security will slow them down. In a Zero Trust world, they don't need to spend a lot of time sacrificing for security. Following a Zero Trust roadmap can protect their systems, valuable intellectual property, and valuable time by minimizing the risk of falling victim to costly breaches.

Here's what small businesses and startups need to include on their Zero Trust roadmaps to reduce the potential for time-consuming, costly breaches that could steal not just data but market momentum too:

- **Put MFA into place for every contractor, admin user, and partner account immediately.** Implementing MFA is highly recommended as it can reduce the risk of privileged access credential abuse.
- **Get a shared account and password vault to reduce the risk of being breached by privileged access abuse.** Password vaults are a must-have for any business that relies on IP, patents, source code under development, and proprietary data that are pivotal to the company's growth. Vaults make sure only trusted applications can request privileged account credentials by first identifying, then validating system accounts before passwords are retrieved. Another major advantage of vaults is that they minimize attack surfaces for small businesses and startups.
- **Secure remote access** needs to be in place to ensure employees, contractor, and IT systems contractors are given least privilege access to

only the resources they need. Small businesses and startups growing fast often don't have the expertise on staff to manage their IT systems. It's cheaper for many to have an IT service that manage server maintenance, upgrades, and security. Secure remote access is predicated on the "never trust, always verify, enforce least privilege" Zero Trust approach to grant access to specific resources.

- **Implement real-time audit and monitoring** to track all privileged sessions and metadata auditing everything across all systems to deliver a comprehensive picture of intentions and outcomes. Creating and adding to an ongoing chronology of login and resource attempts is invaluable for discovering how a security incident first gets started and for meeting compliance requirements. It's much easier to identify and thwart privileged credential abuse based on the insights gained from the single system of record a real-time audit and monitoring service creates. As small businesses and startups grow, the data that real-time audits and monitoring generate are invaluable in proving privileged access is controlled and audited to meet the regulatory compliance requirements of SOX, HIPAA, FISMA, NIST, PCI, MAS, and other regulatory standards.
- **Privileged access credentials to network devices need to be part of the Zero Trust roadmap.** Small businesses and startups face a continual time shortage and sometimes forget to change the manufacturer default passwords, which are often weak and well known in the hacker community. This is why it needs to be a priority to include the network device portfolio in a Zero Trust privilege-based security roadmap and strategy. Security admins need to have these included in the shared account and passwords vault.

For small businesses that are outsourcing IT and security administration, the core elements of the Zero Trust roadmap provide them secure login and a "never trust, always verify, enforce least privilege" strategy that can scale with their business. With Zero Trust privilege, small businesses and startups will be able to grant least privilege access based on verifying who is requesting access, the context of the request, and the risk of the access environment.

1.7.4 Consumers

How can consumers adopt a Zero Trust approach to stay secure? This is an interesting question, as it touches on the consumer versus enterprise Zero Trust concept. Enterprise Zero Trust is much more about "internet first" authentication capabilities, and this question touches more on end-user education, which teaches "trust no one" as a foundational component.

That said, from an education perspective, everyone needs to understand that cyberattacks and scams escalate during particular periods such as holidays. The price of living in a universally connected world is that we are now universally attacked – and the only way to defend against this constant barrage of threats is to adopt a Zero Trust mentality. This means consumers should trust no one and should assume hackers and scammers are on the other end of every form of communications – whether it's emails from UPS, promos on social media, telemarketers asking for charitable donations, or even people knocking on their front door.

A few recommendations given next that consumers can take note of for awareness and prevent a potential attack on your endpoints, email, and internet experience.

- Be aware that phishing attacks are at an all-time high during the holiday season and question any request for personal information that comes over email or online. Bogus shipping emails are particularly common during the holidays.
- Refrain from trusting phone solicitations from charities and businesses because they might be scams. Senior citizens are a favorite target of scammers because they tend to have nest eggs and trust the telephone.
- Closely monitor credit card statements. Assuming credit card numbers have been stolen is a safe bet today, given the number of data breaches that have occurred. Ironically, the sheer number of stolen card numbers is the best protection consumers have today because criminals can't use them all.
- Be suspicious of any "too good to be true" deals on social media, as they could be attempts to direct people to malicious websites or to steal personal information. Travel scams, in particular, proliferate during the holidays.
- Cybercriminals don't just target consumers through their personal contact information and social media profiles; they also go after professional email addresses and accounts. As every employee is a consumer, many employees check their personal accounts on corporate networks, putting their companies at risk.

Everyone should think about adopting Zero Trust habits for personal security, and these habits should be maintained moving forward. In fact, this would be the perfect New Year's resolution for anyone using connected devices. Attacks and scams may spike during the holidays, but they don't end when the ball drops in Times Square. Making Zero Trust a core component of personal security practices can help individuals stay safe from cyberattacks all year round.

1.8 Chapter Summary

- The rise in cyberattacks and ransomware has awakened business leaders all over the world to a new reality. The threats to network and data security have grown beyond what many traditional security solutions can defend against.

- A Zero Trust model assumes that all users or devices can't be trusted until they are verified. When a user or device asks for access to a resource or a network they need to be verified before access can be granted. Zero Trust is one of the most effective ways for organizations to control access to their networks, applications, and data.
- The popular Zero Trust principles are recommended by the NIST, Open Group, Microsoft, and Forrester. Additional principles are also proposed that are perhaps relevant for organizations of all sizes to consider. The organization today has a wide variety of standards and framework to refer to; pick the framework which is best suited for your organization's culture and risk appetite.
- To implement ZTA, organizations need to think about going past the idea of integrating security tools that are supported by the number of organizational security policies in place. Instead, we should look to Zero Trust as a guiding principle that leads to a move towards honest conversation about how our organization is working and what processes and technologies need to be adopted to work more securely.
- The Zero Trust model stipulates that trust should be explicitly derived from a mix of identity and context-based aspects. The name comes about because when it comes to network access, Zero Trust starts with a default deny posture for everyone –government, enterprises, small businesses, and consumers.

References

- 3 Reasons Cyberattacks are Increasing (and How Zero Trust Can Help) (security-intelligence.com)
- https://nvlpubs.nist.gov/nistpubs/SpecialPublications/NIST.SP.800-207.pdf
- Why Your Business Needs to Adopt Zero Trust Principles for Cybersecurity | Corporate Compliance Insights
- Use a zero trust approach to combat IoT security risks – IoT Agenda (techtarget.com)
- How to prevent ransomware attacks with a zero-trust security model – TechRepublic
- Zero-trust initiatives rely on incremental security improvements (techtarget.com)
- DI_2021-TT-zero-trust-never-trust-always-verify.pdf (deloitte.com)
- Did Reagan really coin the term 'Trust but verify,' a proverb revived by HBO's Chernobyl? – Russia Beyond (rbth.com)
- Zero-trust methodology's popularity a double-edged sword (techtarget.com)
- 10 Reasons Why Enterprises Need Zero Trust Security | ColorTokens
- How to prevent ransomware attacks with a zero-trust security model – TechRepublic
- Why consumers must adopt a "zero trust" approach to security [Q&A] (betanews.com)
- Roadmap To Zero Trust for Small Businesses (forbes.com)
- 10 Reasons Why Enterprises Need Zero Trust Security | ColorTokens

- The Open Group Zero Trust Initiative and The President's Executive Order on Improving the Nation's Cybersecurity – The Open Group Blog
- http://aka.ms/zerotrust
- https://publications.opengroup.org/security-library/w210?_ga= 2.60250792.401442715.1629003093-1836687739.1627603702
- https://go.forrester.com/blogs/tag/ztx/

Security can longer scale in the way we have done things for 20+ years. We need a new way of doing things to get leverage in our model. Zero Trust is foundational for the future of every security program. However, Zero Trust is a journey and will not happen overnight.

Jason Clark, Chief Strategy Officer, Netskope

Chapter 2

Zero Trust – Disrupting the Business Model

Gartner estimates 60% of businesses will shift to Zero Trust networks by 2023. A separate global study showed that 42% had plans to adopt a Zero Trust strategy and are in the early implementation phases.

In this chapter, we walk through the business imperatives of Zero Trust and our perspectives on how Zero Trust disrupts the business model today and in the future.

2.1 Why Business Leaders Care about Zero Trust

In the digital era, many traditional industries, capabilities, products, and services have moved online, either as part of enterprise digital evolution or because of new operational needs imposed by COVID in 2020 to 2022. As a result, companies in every industry are going digital. And that puts the topic of security and privacy front and center in the minds of senior executives.

Higher customer (and end-user!) expectations have driven businesses to change to adopt a digital experience. Security and privacy are undergoing a similar evolution, and that's where Zero Trust security philosophy, platforms, and services can impact your business service delivery and change the way you design your brand, customer experience, speed of driving change, ease of doing business, and even reputation.

Network and security architectures from the post-dot-com boom era were designed for stability, rigidity, and control, not the agility needed to support rapid business evolution. They are – by their very nature – the epitome of inflexibility. Increases in data require increases in bandwidth. Is traffic spiking? Add more boxes. Pivot to work from home? Add more boxes. For enterprises running duplicated stacks of security appliances, the ideals of operational accuracy, performance optimization, and business agility remain pipe dreams.

2.1.1 Agility Fuels Digital Transformation

In every industry, new players use agility to disrupt. A Zero Trust architecture delivers agility. And better security. And better performance. Stakeholders

DOI: 10.1201/9781003225096-4

must demand more from business leaders. Would those business leaders look like they do now if they were to design operational infrastructure, workflows, and operations from scratch? And if these leaders could employ a Zero Trust architecture (ZTA) to deliver better security, greater agility, significantly reduced costs, and significantly reduced risk, why wouldn't they?

ZTA allows security to shift focus to shared business objectives. In this way, ZTA can transform IT from "The Ministry of 'No'" to the "Ministry of 'This is How We Get Things Done.'"

Enterprise secure digital transformation using Zero Trust architecture seems an easy choice for an enterprise information technology (IT) organization: better security, better resilience, faster performance, and lower cost. When it comes to digital competition, speed matters, and driving change at warp speed is required. In traditional environments, making any change to legacy demilitarized zone (DMZ) firewall infrastructure is a cumbersome process, restricted to lower-traffic, weekend-only scheduling. Cloud-based ZTA is dynamic, with policy-based security that can be adapted on the fly. You can't afford to change once a month when your evolving digital challengers can deliver change 20 times a day.

Cloud-based ZTA delivers the next evolution of enterprise security. But that simple fact should not obscure its tangible impact on a customer enterprise: ZTA is a *business* solution that delivers *business* benefits.

Enterprise leaders that cling to (or tacitly allow their IT departments to cling to) outdated security models do so at their peril, at significant risk to their livelihood, and at great risk to their organization. In doing so, they limit organizational agility, incur unnecessary overhead, hinder growth, and complicate operational management.

Enterprise leaders who sustain insecurely antiquated infrastructure have a responsibility to either justify outdated practices or modernize. Why is the organization in the network security business? Can it secure its enterprise data, users, assets, and resources better than a cloud-edge service provider with thousands or security experts working 24/7 to block the latest adversarial threats? Can it anticipate the next supply-chain threat? Can it patch instantly?

2.1.2 The New (Reduced) Cost of Doing Business

Organizations adopting ZTA have significantly reduced their reliance on MPLS networks and hardware-based security, which has slashed tens of millions of dollars from IT budgets. It also provided a better (faster) connectivity performance, improved security (with full SSL/TLS inspection), and better mobile-device access, which was particularly valuable when companies shifted to remote work. As a result of increased efficiency, IT staff can concentrate on strategic, business-critical objectives.

Refer to customer case studies given in the chapter 5 to understand how customers reduced costs and improved agility with the adoption of ZTA.

2.1.3 Business Leaders' Commitment to Support Zero Trust Adoption

Business leaders might not understand digital security risk well. Their technical expertise might be limited. They might therefore be hesitant to approve a security-related investment if they don't know what's being proposed.

Knowing this, security leaders might consider framing their dialogue with executives in terms of business risk. They can specifically speak to how a "trust by default" policy opens up the possibility of attackers affecting mission-critical operations and profits. They can then set this in contrast to a Zero Trust model, which supports business objectives. Quantifying the risk may ease your conversation with business leaders to educate them on how ZTA can mitigate organization risk from stolen data, malware, and ransomware attacks.

You won't succeed in putting Zero Trust in place without the requisite budget or support. You have a vested interest in making sure leadership understands what's going on every step of the way. Speaking the language of business, pilot programs, and simple metrics, you can foster a culture of Zero Trust together with the C-Suite, all while retaining the money you need to fulfill your employer's security needs.

2.2 Zero Trust Starts with a Culture

When it comes to Zero Trust, if you're the only one focused on Zero Trust, you will not have much success. It is essential to create a culture that embraces Zero Trust in your organization. This means broadening the conversation. We need to bring everyone in – business leaders, risk management, IT, human resources, finance, you name it. The first question our business leaders must ask is: "What do you mean; we can't trust?" To be successful in running an organization, we need trust. Trust is the currency of business.

Zero Trust isn't about individuals; it's about packets. We can trust an individual, but we don't have to trust the packets attached to that individual through the devices and networks that are the lifeblood of our organization.

Zero Trust is more than an architecture; it's also a philosophy. To change culture, you need a strong, underlying philosophy.

2.2.1 Know Your Organization

Of course, knowing your organization is the fundamental step before you determine the potential business model change that you can anticipate by adopting ZTA. So how do you make sure you are having the right conversations and are building the right culture for Zero Trust? Every organization is different, with diverse digital technologies transforming our workplaces and creating new expectations for users and customers.

For example, in a university, the concept of academic freedom is one of the driving values of higher education. This is critical to protecting the vitality of research. However, suppose any of the faculties think universities should not have firewalls at all because they could be used to monitor users, or they might slow down internet connections. In that case, it points to the fact the organization does not carry a "security first" mindset.

We need to make sure board members and business leaders are focused on cyber risk and, instead of looking at scaling back, they want to make sure we are doing everything possible to enhance protection and mitigate that risk.

2.2.2 Inspire Trust

For years, we have all been saying that security is everyone's job. Zero Trust forces you to put that culture in place to get everyone involved in recognizing that they have a vested interest in securing a role in their community. How do you accomplish this?

It comes down to behaviors – culture can be thought of as how people behave when no one is looking. When we have conversations and work with people, we try to understand their bad behaviors so we can fix them together. It's essential to get your community to rally around a standard message of fixing those day-to-day destructive behaviors that create more risk for the organization.

To break through the barriers of culture, get to know your community. People want to be secure, but you can't lead and change the culture by instilling fear and telling them that the sky is falling all of the time. You can't create a cybersecurity culture from behind your desk; you need to be out there building relationships. You have to develop and inspire trust to succeed with Zero Trust.

2.2.3 Managing Up and Around

Another critical component of building a Zero Trust culture is to manage the organization. The leadership team should be transparent and honest across the board in setting up the goal and managing the expectation of ZTA.

There is a role for every senior leader in the organization to build credibility by answering the question 'why ZTA?' from their peers, superiors and direct reports. By answering this question, you create a level of trust that is a foundation for a Zero Trust culture. Ultimately, if you have conversations with everyone not based on fear but on how we can all work together to make everyone more secure.

2.2.4 A Philosophy of Ownership

Security is foundational to every solution that you build and implement. The organizational structure must adopt a Zero Trust philosophy of ownership and a habit of thinking about security first. One more vital point to understand. Zero Trust is not a one-and-done. That's why we want organizations to consider Zero Trust more as a philosophy than as an architecture. You're never done, and you always have to be reassessing. You have to do ongoing monitoring and analysis. You have to figure out what people are doing and continuously improve your process, policies, and principles.

2.3 Paradigm Shift in the Business Model

A significant paradigm shift occurred in the past few years. Much like other technological shifts of the past decade – when cloud computing changed the way we do business, Agile changed the way we develop software and Amazon changed the way we shop – Zero Trust presents us with a new paradigm in how we secure our organizations, our data and our employees. While difficult to identify the precise tipping point, one thing is certain: what were once extraordinarily high-profile, damaging breaches are no longer extraordinary. In recent years, Yahoo, Accenture, HBO, Verizon, Uber, Equifax, Deloitte, the U.S. SEC, the RNC, the DNC, the OPM, HP, Oracle, and a profusion of attacks aimed at the Small and Medium Business (SMB) market have all proven that every organization – public or private – is susceptible. The epiphany behind the paradigm shift is clear, widely accepted security approaches based on bolstering a trusted network do not work. And they never will. This is primarily when businesses deal with skill shortages, overloaded employees, and an ever-expanding number of cloud apps and mobile devices that broaden the attack surface with each passing day.

The basic principles of securing access to critical information have not changed, but the ecosystem your information resides in has transformed significantly. Changes in business and IT operations have introduced unnecessary complexity and risk to modern enterprises. However, the time has come for organizations to change their approach to security or risk facing the consequences of a cyberattack or data breach.

We are trying to solve new problems with old solutions. Today, users can access sensitive networks from virtually anywhere, and interconnected systems have altered the makeup of our network architectures. Digital transformation initiatives increase attack surfaces and diversify how employees, customers, and partners interact with a given organization. Amidst all of these paradigm shifts in IT, security has not been able to transform accordingly – until now.

We enter the era of Zero Trust, a model based on the idea that no identity (user or machine) should be inherently trusted. Zero Trust is quickly being adopted by progressive security teams who understand the need to take a different approach to secure access to data. The principles of secure access do not change; the paradigm shift is in how they are achieved.

Security leaders can discuss a plan for using a Zero Trust model with business decision makers. They might consider staying away from changing the entire network over a short period of time. After all, the business leaders want to make sure that their budget decisions will bring value to the group. A good compromise might be a pilot program for using Zero Trust within a specific part of the network.

The security team can use that engagement to track what worked and what didn't and demonstrate the value of Zero Trust. If this works, executives might be much more willing to expand Zero Trust across the whole system.

You can also foster that connection by using benchmarks, visuals, and other metrics that are easy to understand from a business perspective. For example, you might demonstrate the time and money saved on not resetting users' credentials so often because of implementing single sign-on (SSO) and other security controls that complement Zero Trust.

2.4 Zero Trust Security Is Vital for Hybrid Work

The COVID-19 pandemic forced all industries to radically shift their operations into more distributed networks to support remote work. As a result, the era of working from an office five days a week is long gone. As businesses continue to embrace working remotely, new approaches to cohesive business functions will also bring about new threats. In fact, companies today are likely facing more security risks than ever before. As a result of these distributed business models, employees access mission-critical IT networks, data, applications, and other confidential information from countless different sources and devices. While this flexibility is favorable for employees, it has also created new opportunities for emerging security threats, challenges, and attacks. It became increasingly clear as organizations accelerated their migration from physical domains and legacy technologies to flexible and agile cloud technologies during the COVID-19 pandemic that convenience, flexibility, and cost savings would become established benefits of remote work and a distributed workforce.

With some users working remotely and others in group office settings, the hybrid work environment introduces more digital attack surfaces, complexity, and risk as perimeters are now increasingly fluid. This shift of the global workforce looks to be a permanent change. Gallup found that nearly two-thirds of U.S. remote workers would like to continue working remotely. And organizations like it, too, with Gartner reporting that 90% of human resources leaders planned on allowing remote work even after the COVID-19 vaccine was available.

As such, a Zero Trust strategy will be top of mind for many organizations because its principles help maintain security amid the IT complexity that comes with hybrid work.

But the shift also comes with a mandate. IT teams need to do more than enable work for anyone, from anywhere; they must ensure that it's secure. That's no small task. At a time with reports of security threats increasing by 400% compared to pre-pandemic levels, IT teams must be more prepared than ever. It's no surprise that organizations of all sizes strengthen their security posture by moving to a Zero Trust model.

Ensuring good cyber hygiene for employees is simplified in an office setting, and all connected devices are on a secure network under the IT department's supervision. However, with a distributed office setup, organizations can't control which networks and devices their employees use to access company data and information.

If your employees work from remote locations, how can you establish contextual relationships with them to ensure they're who they say they are? How do you validate the devices and applications they're using to connect to your systems and data? How can you ensure that the networks they're connecting to are secure? The differences between working from an office setting versus a personal network or public Wi-Fi at a coffee shop or train station can be the silver bullet for a bad actor trying to override an organization's security measures.

Companies have never been more vulnerable. Organizations should implement a Zero Trust strategy to galvanize their security and better defend their digital assets from emerging threats and attacks in the new telecommuting world. And to guarantee success, they must provide a simplified user experience for their employees.

- **How Zero Trust thwarts bad actors**. Zero Trust security is essentially an ongoing verification process whenever a device tries to obtain access or connect to a business' network. Through this approach, companies are better positioned to defend against the leading causes of security breaches – including user impersonation, password reuse, data breaches, and stolen credentials – by analyzing various pieces of information to confirm one's identity before granting access to the network. This can include a combination of numerous strategies, such as the micro-segmentation of networks, authentication of users, and verification of a secure network.

  By implementing Zero Trust security, companies can do away with standard password protection, one of the leading causes of phishing schemes. Simultaneously, they can ensure greater user privacy – granting peace of mind for the company and its employees.

- **How automation ensures success**. Enterprise security isn't typically top of mind for employees. As employees continue to juggle the demands of adapting to remote work, there's increased room for oversights. Unfortunately, oversights in cyber hygiene can be exceptionally costly – or even disastrous – for a company. So, it's in an organization's best interest to ensure these security measures also provide a fantastic user experience for their employees (and cause minimal interruption to their workdays). To achieve this, companies can instead implement these enhanced security measures via automation rather than training staff individually on best practices for their devices or networks.

By automating and enforcing security measures and protocols, companies can utilize deep learning capabilities and other emerging technologies to help detect potential challenges, such as device performance issues, security vulnerabilities, and application crashes. This enables them to correct these issues remotely before impacting the end user. Access to this intelligence can help organizations maintain operational awareness across all devices, no matter where employees are signing in from – keeping all parties safe.

- **Zero Trust with zero exceptions.** Disruption brings about innovation – but innovations in remote work have also brought about innovations in hacks and other cyberattacks. However, organizations can ensure business-critical information remains private and secure by implementing a Zero Trust security strategy.

  What's more, automating these strategies allows companies to keep the heavy lifting of security maintenance theirs and not the personal responsibility of their employees. This approach ensures that they can remain focused on their roles and that business can continue to run smoothly and securely with limited interruptions – no matter what location a team member connects from.

2.5 Human Elements of Zero Trust

Security specialists have long known that a single weak link in a chain is all that is needed to bring down a cyberdefense. Sometimes this comes down to an errant line of code in a hastily developed application programming interface (API), inadequate penetration testing, or old, unpatched, exploitable code hidden deep within a legacy system. But more often than not, it is because of the actions of one individual – a single person who clicks on a malware payload within a phishing email, who allows an individual to physically access a workplace unchallenged, or whose work-from-home office features a Wi-Fi router that was never properly secured.

Awareness of malicious and threat actors has encouraged most organizations to rank cybersecurity ever higher in priority, but in many cases, there remains the belief that data and activities occurring inside the fortress walls are safe by virtue of their being on the inside. This, of course, is erroneous and has given rise to the Zero Trust model, in which all activities, including those occurring within the security perimeter, are to be held to the same standard of trust, which is zero.

This is a welcome leap forward in cybersecurity and helps dispense with the notion that threat actors only attack their targets directly, when in truth, they are more likely to find a weak entry point and then move laterally across a network. But a Zero Trust protocol is still just a set of rules and procedures and again falls prey to human weakness in the form of errors, incompetence and – most ironically of all – trust to allow the system to fail again.

There is no security without human elements. Humans decide the security priority, policy, and procedure. They instrument and implement those to secure their environment. What is ironic is, the human element determines the robust strategy for their most valuable assets but also introduces risk to the same environment. Buying a software or tool is an easy part but operationalizing it and getting it used in the right way is the most important step to bring value from the investment they made. That relies on the human element.

Let us go a little deeper into the human elements by looking at the security leadership (chief information officer [CIO]), security professionals, skills, and employees and determine the potential role they could play in successfully adopting the ZTA.

2.5.1 Role of the Chief Information Officer

Zero Trust represents an opportunity to move away from the "department of no" label to become an enabler of business transformation for CIOs and the security teams that report to them. To get the Zero Trust journey underway, CIOs should:

- **Position Zero Trust as a foundational business initiative, not a security project.** In addition to the business benefits arising from improved security and lower risk, Zero Trust puts in place an essential building block for any analytics initiative an organization might wish to embark upon: the understanding of what data you've got, where it resides, and who can handle it for what purpose.
- **Align with the chief information security officer (CISO) around Zero Trust.** CISOs and CIOs typically have different objectives and incentives, which can lead to conflict and finger-pointing. Zero Trust allows CIOs and CISOs to work toward a common goal and give the CISO a stronger story to share with the board. However, CISOs should report to the chief executive officer, not the CIO; whether perceived or real, a CIO reporting line leads to a potential lack of transparency, which in turn can increase business risk.

- **Refuse to take "no" for an answer.** There are no legitimate business objections to a Zero Trust approach. You're not proposing to embark upon a potentially risky and costly rip-and-replace exercise; you'll be using off-the-shelf tools and existing skills. In other words, over time, you'll break the seemingly endless upward spiral of security expenditure and instead lower costs – but with much improved security.

2.5.2 Role of Security Professionals

One key human element is how security professionals can help accelerate the adoption of ZTA in the organization. Security professionals can play the role of an advocate to embrace the values of Zero Trust by the following ways

- Encourage to adopt a Zero Trust mindset – to adequately address the modern dynamic threat environment requires.
  - Coordinated and aggressive system monitoring, system management, and defensive operations capabilities
  - Assuming all requests for critical resources and all network traffic may be malicious
  - Assuming all devices and infrastructure may be compromised
  - Accepting that all access approvals to critical resources incur risk and preparing to perform rapid damage assessment, control, and recovery operations
- Embrace the Zero Trust guiding principles.
- Leverage Zero Trust design concepts.
- Share best practices.

2.5.3 Using a Zero Trust Framework to Solve the Skills Gap

In July 2020, Deloitte surveyed webinar attendees about its organization's plans to implement a Zero Trust model. The poll found that four challenges had disrupted the efforts of many employers. A lack of skilled workers garnered the most attention at 28.3%. Close behind was a lack of needed budget at 28.1% followed by lack of discernment in getting started (12.8%) and being unable to choose between technologies or vendors in the market (12.7%).

Luckily, these challenges don't have to stand in the way of teams adopting a Zero Trust security model. They can implement steps to address each of the challenges referenced above.

Organizations find themselves with a problem because of the skills gap. On the one hand, they realize their network infrastructure suffers from a human flaw: the emotion of trust.

Increasingly more organizations are recognizing trust doesn't inherently belong in the network. They're beginning to look to the Zero Trust security model as a way to remove unneeded trust.

On the other hand, organizations struggle to find talented personnel who can manage trust across their IT systems. They might lack the skilled workforce needed to remove some sources of trust and preserve others. Because of this, they might feel the Zero Trust model doesn't fit their needs.

Luckily, there's a way forward. Organizations don't have to rely on internal expertise to put Zero Trust in place. They can instead invest in vendor solutions that rely on artificial intelligence and machine learning to keep customers secure. With the help of a managed security service provider, organizations can draw upon the expertise of external experts in shaping the way their systems manage trust.

Of course, organizations would need to be able to find a Zero Trust solution that is customizable and serves their security needs. They also need to make sure they have the security budget to accommodate this tool. Much of this advice boils down to asking prospective vendors the right types of questions about their solutions.

For now, organizations that are strapped for skilled personnel need to realize the skills gap hasn't trapped them. Now is the time for them to begin exploring the vendor landscape for solutions that can help them put Zero Trust in place.

2.5.4 Role of Employees

For organizations to truly benefit from a Zero Trust model in remote work, the same mindset must be brought into the home by their employees. Whether they're accessing the internet for work or personal reasons, users need to apply a Zero Trust approach that keeps the wrong people out. And it's more than just security awareness training or a strong password policy. Users at home should constantly be questioning every interaction online, including emails and texts with links and communications that seem out of character by the sender even if it appears to come from an official source. Phishing attempts and other attacks rely heavily on complacency, so a Zero Trust requires vigilance out of habit.

These habits and overall mindset are essential to successfully applying a Zero Trust approach to security in the organization, regardless of where employees are working. Having the right technology is a critical enabler, but you need the right governance policies and employee engagement if you're to secure your business fully.

2.6 Chapter Summary

- Higher customer (and end-user!) expectations have driven businesses to adopt a digital experience. Security and privacy are undergoing a similar evolution, and that's where Zero Trust security philosophy, platforms, and services can impact your business service delivery, and change the way you design your brand, customer experience, speed of driving change, ease of doing business, and even reputation.

- It is essential to create a culture that embraces Zero Trust in your organization. We need to bring everyone in – business leaders, risk management, IT, human resources, finance, you name it.
- A significant paradigm shift occurred in the past few years. The COVID-19 pandemic forced all industries to radically shift their operations into more distributed networks to support remote work. As a result, the era of working from an office five days a week is long gone. As such, a Zero Trust strategy will be top of mind for many organizations because its principles help maintain security amid the IT complexity that comes with hybrid work.
- There is no security without human elements. Humans decide the security priority, policy, and procedure. They instrument and implement those to secure their environment. By looking at the security leadership (CIO), security professionals, skills, and employees to determine the potential role they could play in successfully adopting the ZTA.

References

- How to Talk to Leadership About a Zero Trust Model That's Right For You (securityintelligence.com)
- wp-zero-trust.pdf (ciosummits.com)
- Why The "New Normal" Requires Zero Trust (forbes.com)
- Why Bet Your Business on Zero Trust Security? | Zscaler
- How to secure your hybrid work world with a Zero Trust approach | Microsoft Security Blog
- Work From Anywhere, Get Hacked From Anywhere: Why Zero Trust Security Is Vital For Remote Work (forbes.com)
- Remote Work Drives Zero Trust Security Adoption – SupraITS
- CloudTweaks | The Human Element of Zero Trust
- Zero Trust Security: A CIO's Guide To Defending Their Business From Cyberattacks | Akamai
- How Zero Trust Can Help Close the Cybersecurity Skills Gap (securityintelligence.com)

Part 2

Current Status and Best Practices of the Zero Trust Journey

Zero Trust is just as much a business enabler as it is a security paradigm.

Zero Trust enables business agility – without Zero Trust, secure cloud consumption is but a pipedream.

Brett James, Director, Transformation Strategy for Zscaler

Chapter 3

Zero Trust Maturity and Implementation Assessment

3.1 Need for a Zero Trust Maturity Model

Implementing Zero Trust takes time and effort; it's a marathon and not a sprint. You cannot achieve a "matured" stage overnight. For many organizations and networks, existing infrastructure can be leveraged and integrated to incorporate Zero Trust concepts, but the transition to a matured Zero Trust architecture (ZTA) often requires additional capabilities to obtain the full benefits of a Zero Trust environment.

From a security maturity perspective, one of the essential things to do is to understand which stage you are and where you want to be.

An organization needs to understand its current stage and plan out the next steps journey for its ZTA journey. Transitioning to a mature ZTA all at once is also unnecessary and not recommended. An organization must incorporate Zero Trust functionality incrementally as part of a strategic plan, which can reduce risk accordingly at each step.

As the Zero Trust implementation matures over time, enhanced visibility and automated responses allow defenders to keep pace with the threat. Zero Trust efforts should be planned as a continually evolving roadmap, from initial preparation to basic, intermediate, and matured stages, with cybersecurity protection, response, and operations improving over time.

Different organizational requirements, existing technology implementations, and security stages affect how a Zero Trust security model is planned out.

3.2 Our Unique Approach to a Zero Trust Maturity Model

Using our experience in helping customers secure their organization and along with the partnership of Deakin University in Australia, we've developed the following maturity model to help you assess your Zero Trust readiness and build a plan to move to the next level of your Zero Trust journey.

We have also taken inspiration from multiple sources to develop this maturity model; some of these sources are Microsoft's ZT Maturity model,

DOI: 10.1201/9781003225096-6

Netskope's Zero Trust Data Protection model, Forrester ZTX Maturity model, and the National Institute of Standards and Technology's 800–207 Zero Trust architecture, to name a few.

Table 3.1 provides an overview of the various levels and their definitions and a few notable characteristics.

At the first stage, you probably want to take advantage of things that you might already have. After you're past the basic level, you want to move into the intermediate level.

The intermediate level is when you might start to think about things such as micro-segmentation. Instead of giving a user access to an entire system, you're giving a user access only to the applications or capabilities on that system that you want them to have access to, specific to data, specific to applications, maybe even containers. So, segmentation is a great place to start, except you will define it perhaps a little bit more

Table 3.1 Definitions and Characteristics of Our Zero Trust Model

Level	Definition and Characteristics
Basic: Level 1	Most of the organization will be at this stage during the start of their Zero Trust journey. At this level, fundamental integrated capabilities are implemented. The strategy here is to start small and focus on strategic wins. **Notable characteristics are:** • On-premises identity management • Basic identity protection and limited multi-factor authentication (MFA) • No device information and visibility • No real-time threat updates and analytics • No data classification • Flat network infrastructure • The resources are primarily on-premises with basic use of cloud capabilities.
Intermediate: Level 2	At the advanced level, the capabilities are further integrated and refined. The strategy for this level is to advance the Zero Trust journey with more robust identity management, data security, and advanced threat detection and response capabilities. **Notable characteristics are:** • Device visibility using mobile device management (MDM) and Domain joined • Real-time threat updates • On-prem security information and event management (SIEM) in place • Identity protection using MFA for critical applications • Fixed policy authorization at the session initiation level • Data access governance is based on perimeter access and not based on data sensitivity • On-premises applications are accessed via VPN or via physical networks appliances

Level	Definition and Characteristics
Matured: **Level 3**	At this matured level, organizations have deployed advanced protection and controls with robust analytics and orchestration. The strategy for this level is to complete and extend Zero Trust principles across advance threat intelligence, threat hunting, advance automation at the security operation center (SOC), and seamless access for the end users. **Notable characteristics are:** • Chief information security officers and chief information officers focus on consolidating point products and vendors to address each Zero Trust component • Granular micro-perimeters and controls around data and application limiting the blast radius • Implementation of MFA of all identities and usage of privilege identity management and access management solutions to manage privilege users • All data are classified based on sensitivity or criticality; data ownership is well defined • Threat telemetry is used to force reauthorization such as time and location • User to internal application traffic is encrypted • All workload is assigned with app identity • Implementation of data loss prevention across all the points • SIEM and SOC process are well defined and leverage cloud capabilities, and advanced analytics features such as User Behaviour Entity Analysis (UBEA) are in use

specifically because at present, it may not be as widely deployed as you want it to be.

Things such as multi-factor authentication can also come in at this stage when you're able to also prevent people from gaining access unless they automatically log in with two-factor authentication; for example, they can't have access to an asset unless stronger authentication mechanisms are used, increasing the level assurance (or confidence) you have in that identity.

And then, finally, in the matured level, you might want to start taking advantage of things such as threat intelligence, security automation, and orchestration. So, this way, instead of simply relying on internal information, the user, and the asset;' you're now bridging that gap and combining external information such as threat intelligence to dictate whether someone should be able to get to something. And if the circumstances are right, they're allowed to, but if they're not, you can take advantage of that automation and orchestration to force them to re-log on to prevent them from having access at all or forcing them to use a two-factor code before they have access to that particular system. And if something happens, you automatically launch processes to get more insight into that action.

While a Zero Trust security model is most effective when integrated across the entire digital estate, most organizations need to take a phased approach that targets specific areas for change based on their Zero Trust maturity, available resources, and priorities. It is essential to consider each investment carefully and align it with current business needs.

The first step of your journey does not have to be a significant lift and shift to cloud-based security tools. Many organizations will benefit significantly from utilizing the hybrid infrastructure that helps you use your existing investments and begin to realize the value of Zero Trust initiatives more quickly.

Fortunately, each step forward will make a difference in reducing risk and returning trust in the entirety of your digital estate.

3.2.1 Zero Trust Cybersecurity Maturity Assessment Toolkit

Zero Trust Cybersecurity Maturity (ZTCM) Assessment Toolkit is a comprehensive worksheet to assess a company's Zero Trust cybersecurity maturity level. It consists of three major elements as described earlier, a self-assessment questionnaire, your self-evaluation scores, and your results with visualization. The survey questionnaire comprises 51 questions across 8 main domains, as follows:

- **Identities**: Whether they represent people, services, or Internet of Things (IoT) devices, identities define the Zero Trust control plane. When an identity attempts to access a resource, we need to verify that identity with strong authentication based on all available data points, including user identity, location, device health, service or workload, data classification, and anomalies.
- **Endpoints and devices**: Once an identity has been granted access to a resource, data can flow to a variety of different devices – from IoT devices to smartphones, bring your own device to partner managed devices, and on-premises workloads to cloud hosted servers. This diversity creates a massive attack surface area, requiring us to monitor and enforce device health and compliance for secure access.
- **Applications and workload**: Applications, workloads, and Application Programming Interfaces (APIs) provide the interface by which data is consumed. They may be legacy on-premises, lift and shift to cloud workloads, or modern software as a service application. Controls and technologies should be applied to discover shadow information technology, ensure appropriate in-app permissions, gate access based on real-time analytics, monitor for abnormal behavior, control user actions, and validate secure configuration options.

- **Data**: Ultimately, security teams are focused on protecting data. When possible, data should remain safe even if it leaves the devices, apps, infrastructure, and networks the organization controls. Data should be classified, labeled, and encrypted, and access should be restricted based on these attributes.
- **Infrastructure**: Whether on-premises servers, cloud-based virtual machines (VMs), containers, or micro services, infrastructure represents a critical threat vector. Assess version, configuration, and just-in-time access to harden defense; use telemetry to detect attacks and anomalies; and automatically block and flag risky behavior and take protective actions.
- **Networks**: All data are ultimately accessed over network infrastructure. Networking controls can provide critical "in-pipe" controls to enhance visibility and help prevent attackers from moving laterally across the network. Networks should be segmented (including deeper in-network micro-segmentation), and real-time threat protection, end-to-end encryption, monitoring, and analytics should be employed.
- **Visibility and analytics**: Analytics enable you to detect punctures, leaks, and pressure points that threaten the flow, integrity, and containment of your sensitive data. Most important, analytics enable you to do something about it – to convert observation into action such as preventing a breach.
- **Automation and orchestration**: Security automation and orchestration are critical to streamlining alert investigation and remediation. Response to common incidents, such as denying access to infected devices, request for additional verification, and so on, should be automated to improve response times and reduce risk exposure. Incident response teams should have artificial intelligence–driven alert management capabilities with automated remediation capabilities to deliver streamlined, end-to-end threat resolution (Figure 3.1).
- **Security policy engines**: A security policy engine is used to make access decisions at critical checkpoints – such as access to networks, apps, and data. Most organizations rely on multiple policy engines spread throughout their environment (e.g., apps, networks, infrastructure). Regardless of location, policy engines should use every possible signal source (including identity, application, device, risk analysis, threat intelligence, and more) to make adaptive access decisions based on real-time risk analysis.

Conceptually, Netskope diagrammatically describes risk context as shown in Figure 3.2.

We will discuss Azure Active Directory Condition Access as a policy engine in detail in our next chapter, which will be focused on the Identity as a key control plane.

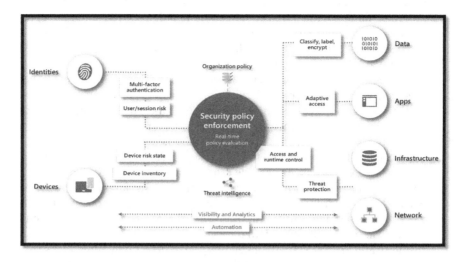

Figure 3.1 Elements and tenets of Zero Trust.

Figure 3.2 Netskope, Risk Context, 2020.

3.2.2 How to Use the Zero Trust Cybersecurity Maturity Assessment Tool?

1   Enter your answer in the specified cell next to each question. Each question needs to be answered with any number from 1 to 5 on the Likert scale (1 = completely disagree, 2 = somewhat disagree, 3 = neither agree nor disagree, 4 = somewhat agree, 5 = completely agree).

2   Visual charts for each domain are automatically generated after you have answered the questions.

3   Get your overall scores and assessment report on the "Report" tab.

4   To download this tool, please visit the following link: *https://github.com/akudrati/ZTBook* (Figures 3.3 and 3.4).

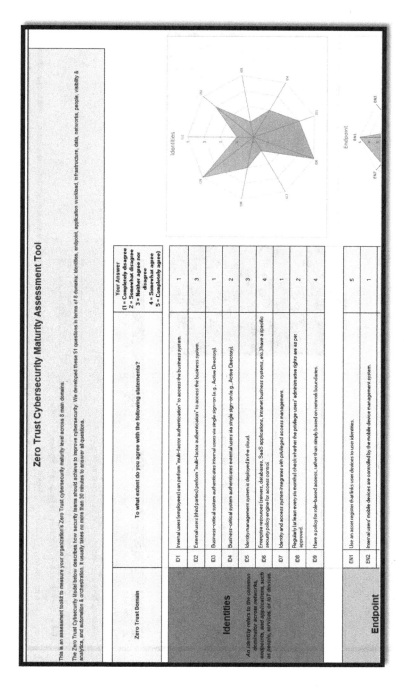

Figure 3.3 Questionnaire tab of the Zero Trust maturity assessment tool.

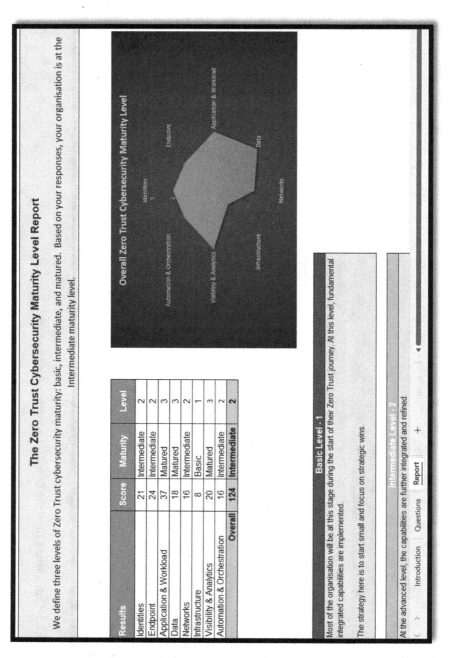

Figure 3.4 Report tab of the Zero Trust maturity assessment tool.

3.3 Microsoft's Three-Stage Maturity Model

Microsoft's three-stage maturity model categorizes organizations into three levels: **traditional, advanced,** and **optimal** (Figure 3.5).

Let's explore each stage of the maturity model against Microsoft's six elements of Zero Trust (Table 3.2).

A further detailed white paper on the Microsoft Maturity Model can be found at https://aka.ms/zerotrust.

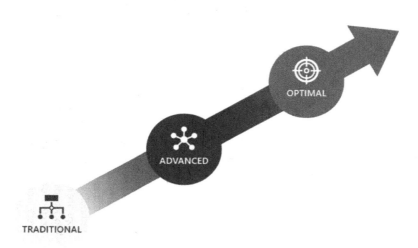

Figure 3.5 Microsoft's Zero Trust maturity model stages.

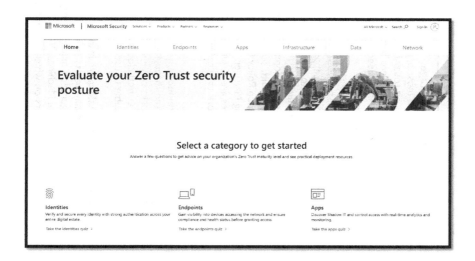

Figure 3.6 Microsoft ZT Security's posture assessment online portal.

Table 3.2 Comparison of the Maturity Model with Microsoft's Six Elements of Zero Trust

Zero Trust Element	Traditional Stage This is when most organizations generally sit today if they haven't started their Zero Trust journey.	Advanced Stage In this stage, organizations have begun their Zero Trust journey and are making progress in a few key areas.	Optimal Stage Organizations in the optimal stage have made large improvements in security.
Identities	• On-premises identity provider is in use. • No single sign-on (SSO) is present between cloud and on-premises apps. • Visibility into identity risk is very limited.	• Cloud identity federates with on-premises system. • Conditional access policies gate access and provide remediation actions. • Analytics improve visibility.	• Password less authentication is enabled. • User, device, location, and behavior are analyzed in real time to determine risk and deliver ongoing protection.
Devices	• Devices are domain joined and managed with solutions such as Group Policy Object or Config Manager. • Devices are required to be on network to access data.	• Devices are registered with cloud identity provider. • Access only granted to cloud-managed and -compliant devices. • Data loss prevention policies are enforced for bring your own devices (BYOD) and corporate devices.	• Endpoint threat detection is used to monitor device risk. • Access control is gated on device risk for both corporate devices and BYOD.
Apps	• On-premises apps are accessed through physical networks or VPN. • Some critical cloud apps are accessible to users.	• On-premises apps are internet-facing and cloud apps are configured with SSO. • Cloud Shadow information technology risk is assessed; critical apps are monitored and controlled.	• All apps are available using least privilege access with continuous verification. • Dynamic control is in place for all apps with in-session monitoring and response.
Infrastructure	• Permissions are managed manually across environments. • Configuration management of Virtual Machines (VMs) and servers on which workloads are running.	• Workloads are monitored and alerted for abnormal behavior. • Every workload is assigned app identity. • Human access to resources requires just-in-time access.	• Unauthorized deployments are blocked, and an alert is triggered. • Granular visibility and access control are available across all workloads. • User and resource access is segmented for each workload

Network	• There are few network security perimeters and flat open network • There is minimal threat protection and static traffic filtering. • Internal traffic is not encrypted,	• There are many ingress and egresses cloud micro-perimeters with some micro-segmentation. • Cloud native filtering and protection is used for known threats. • User-to-app internal traffic is encrypted.	• There are fully distributed ingress and egress cloud micro-perimeters and deeper micro-segmentation. • Machine Learning (ML)-based threat protection and filtering with context-based signals are used. • All traffic is encrypted.
Data	• Access is governed by perimeter control, not data sensitivity. • Sensitivity labels are applied manually, with inconsistent data classification.	• Data are classified and labeled via regex or keyword methods. • Access decisions are governed by encryption.	• Classification is augmented by smart machine learning models. • Access decisions are governed by a cloud security policy engine. • DLP policies secure sharing with encryption and tracking

To get a better understanding of your organization's control gaps, you must also look at Microsoft's Maturity Assessment Tool; this online assessment tool can be found at https://aka.ms/zerotrust (Figure 3.6).

Our opinion: What we like about the Microsoft model is that this model is simple to understand, easy to follow, and the complement assessment portal helps provide control by control gaps with reference to Microsoft technologies.

If you are heavily invested in Microsoft technology, then we highly recommend you try the online assessment portal to identify the current gaps in your organization and leverage the Zero Trust assessment template available as a part of the Data Protection Baseline template in Microsoft Compliance Manager; see the details in Section 3.3.1.

3.3.1 Zero Trust Assessment Using Microsoft Compliance Manager

Who doesn't like automation? Well, here is the latest update from Microsoft. Now you can use Microsoft Compliance Manager to assess Zero Trust maturity and create a dashboard for ongoing progress monitoring.

3.3.1.1 First Thing First: What Is Compliance Manager?

Microsoft Compliance Manager is a feature in the Microsoft 365 compliance center that helps you manage your organization's compliance requirements with greater ease and convenience. Compliance Manager can help you throughout your compliance journey, from taking inventory of your data protection risks to managing the complexities of implementing controls, staying current with regulations and certifications, and reporting to auditors.

To access the compliance manager, visit https://compliance.microsoft.com.

3.3.1.2 Zero Trust Integration for the Data Protection Baseline Template

Zero Trust is a proactive, integrated approach to security across all layers of the digital estate that explicitly and continuously verifies every transaction; asserts least privilege; and relies on intelligence, advanced detection, and real-time response to threats. Compliance Manager's Data Protection Baseline template, included for all users, now integrates 57 new controls and 36 new actions for Zero Trust aligned across the following control families:

- Zero Trust Application
- Zero Trust App development guidance
- Zero Trust Endpoint
- Zero Trust Data

- Zero Trust Identity
- Zero Trust Infrastructure
- Zero Trust Network
- Zero Trust Visibility, Automation, and Orchestration

The new and updated Data Protection Baseline template now includes Zero Trust control families. These control families map to existing and additional improvement actions, making it easy to assess, monitor, and improve compliance with our Zero Trust principles and recommendations.

Admins can use data protection baseline to implement actions that can enable them to follow a Zero Trust strategy by leveraging the improvement actions in the newly added Zero Trust control families that map to Zero Trust areas of Apps, Data, Endpoint, Identity, Infrastructure, and Network.

Follow these steps to review and assess your organization.

1   Visit https://compliance.microsoft.com.
2   Select Assessment Template.
3   Select Data Protection Baseline template.
4   Create a new assessment as shown in Figure 3.7.

After the assessment is created, select the newly created template, and filter the controls with Zero Trust domain as shown in Figure 3.8.

Continue to add your implementation detail as per required domain, and you will see your score on the main dashboard based on control implementation status.

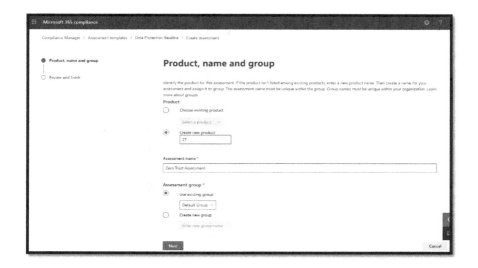

Figure 3.7 Microsoft 365 Compliance Manager Assessment Template creation screenshot.

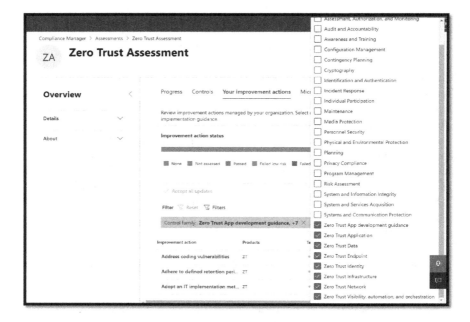

Figure 3.8 Microsoft 365 Compliance Manager Zero Trust Assessment creation screenshot.

3.4 CISA's Zero Trust Maturity Model

Cybersecurity & Infrastructure Security Agency (CISA)'s Zero Trust Maturity Model is one of many roadmaps for agencies to reference as it transitions toward a ZTA.

The goal of the maturity model is to assist agencies in developing their Zero Trust strategies and implementation plans and present ways in which various CISA services can support Zero Trust solutions across agencies.

The maturity model, which includes five pillars and three cross-cutting capabilities, is based on the foundations of Zero Trust. The maturity model provides agencies with specific examples of a traditional, advanced, and optimal Zero Trust architecture within each pillar (Figure 3.9).

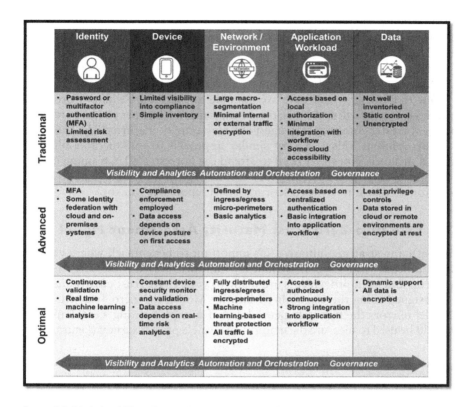

Identity	Device	Network / Environment	Application Workload	Data
Traditional				
• Password or multifactor authentication (MFA) • Limited risk assessment	• Limited visibility into compliance • Simple inventory	• Large macro-segmentation • Minimal internal or external traffic encryption	• Access based on local authorization • Minimal integration with workflow • Some cloud accessibility	• Not well inventoried • Static control • Unencrypted
Visibility and Analytics Automation and Orchestration Governance				
Advanced				
• MFA • Some identity federation with cloud and on-premises systems	• Compliance enforcement employed • Data access depends on device posture on first access	• Defined by ingress/egress micro-perimeters • Basic analytics	• Access based on centralized authentication • Basic integration into application workflow	• Least privilege controls • Data stored in cloud or remote environments are encrypted at rest
Visibility and Analytics Automation and Orchestration Governance				
Optimal				
• Continuous validation • Real time machine learning analysis	• Constant device security monitor and validation • Data access depends on real-time risk analytics	• Fully distributed ingress/egress micro-perimeters • Machine learning-based threat protection • All traffic is encrypted	• Access is authorized continuously • Strong integration into application workflow	• Dynamic support • All data is encrypted
Visibility and Analytics Automation and Orchestration Governance				

Figure 3.9 High-level Zero Trust Maturity Model by CISA.

Source: www.cisa.gov/publication/zero-trust-maturity-model

For a detailed white paper on CISA's approach, visit www.cisa.gov/publication/zero-trust-maturity-model.

Our opinion: This is another simple and easy to understand approach; however, it is not very comprehensive, and it covers details relating to five key domains of ZT.

3.5 Forrester's ZTX Security Maturity Model

To implement a secure Zero Trust eXtended (ZTX) ecosystem, you must first assess your security maturity.

Forrester's report, Gauge Your ZTX Security Maturity, will help you evaluate how your operations stand against six key competencies of the ZTX ecosystem, which include **Data, Networks, People, Workload, Device, Analytics, and Automation.**

CISOs and security leaders should prioritize taking inventory of their ZTX ecosystem to implement an effective and cohesive strategy.

Due to copyright issues, we are not able to share the detail of Forrester's ZTX Security Maturity Model; the detailed approach paper can be purchased www.forrester.com/report/gauge-your-ztx-security-maturity/RES136187.

Our opinion: This is a very similar approach to our methodology. To access this tool, you either need to attend the Forrester ZTX training or buy the approach paper using the tool mentioned earlier. What we like about this tool is that it provides a scoring-based report like our tool.

3.6 Palo Alto Zero Trust Maturity Assessment Model

As with any strategic initiative, it's important to benchmark where you are as you begin your Zero Trust journey and measure your maturity as time goes on and as improvements are made to your Zero Trust environment.

Designed using the Capability Maturity Model, the Zero Trust Maturity Model mirrors the five-step methodology for implementing Zero Trust and should be used to measure the maturity of a single protect surface (Figure 3.10).

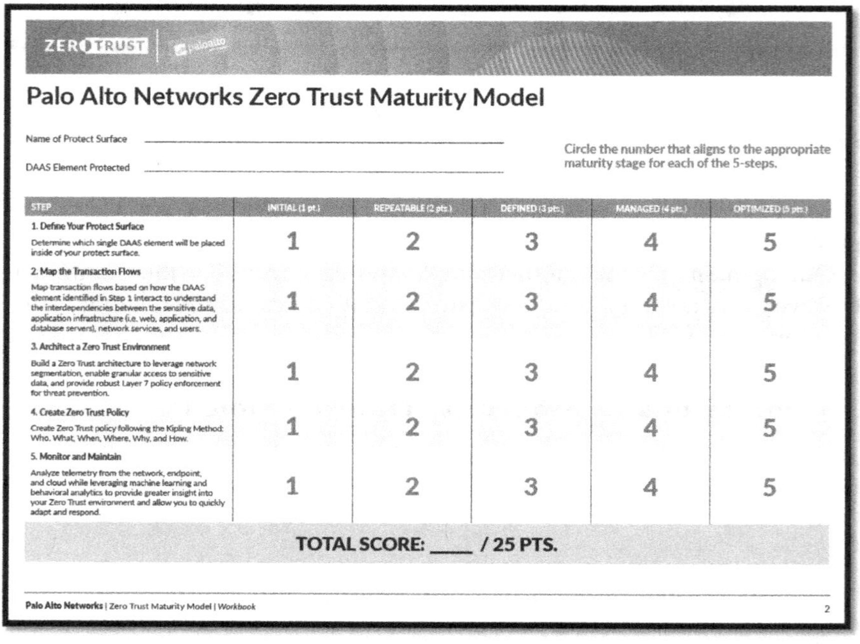

Palo Alto Networks Zero Trust Maturity Model

Name of Protect Surface _____
DAAS Element Protected _____

Circle the number that aligns to the appropriate maturity stage for each of the 5-steps.

STEP	INITIAL (1 pt.)	REPEATABLE (2 pts.)	DEFINED (3 pts.)	MANAGED (4 pts.)	OPTIMIZED (5 pts.)
1. Define Your Protect Surface Determine which single DAAS element will be placed inside of your protect surface.	1	2	3	4	5
2. Map the Transaction Flows Map transaction flows based on how the DAAS element identified in Step 1 interact to understand the interdependencies between the sensitive data, application infrastructure (i.e. web, application, and database servers), network services, and users.	1	2	3	4	5
3. Architect a Zero Trust Environment Build a Zero Trust architecture to leverage network segmentation, enable granular access to sensitive data, and provide robust Layer 7 policy enforcement for threat prevention.	1	2	3	4	5
4. Create Zero Trust Policy Create Zero Trust policy following the Kipling Method: Who, What, When, Where, Why, and How.	1	2	3	4	5
5. Monitor and Maintain Analyze telemetry from the network, endpoint, and cloud while leveraging machine learning and behavioral analytics to provide greater insight into your Zero Trust environment and allow you to quickly adapt and respond.	1	2	3	4	5

TOTAL SCORE: ____ / 25 PTS.

Palo Alto Networks | Zero Trust Maturity Model | Workbook   2

Figure 3.10 Palo Alto scoring method for Zero Trust maturity assessment.

A detailed paper on the Palo Alto approach can be downloaded from www.paloaltonetworks.com/resources/guides/zero-trust-maturity-model.

Our opinion: If you want assessment your organization from a networking point of view, then the Palo Aalto scoring method can provide you an easy and quantifiable score against the networking domain of Zero Trust. Use this method in combination with any assessment approach.

3.7 Chapter Summary

* An organization must integrate Zero Trust across the digital estate to gain the Zero Trust security model to gain the maximum advantage Zero Trust security model. You will be required to adopt a phased approach that targets a specific tenet of Zero Trust, available resources, and priorities.
* It is essential to consider each investment carefully and align them with current business needs. The first step of your journey does not have to be a significant lift and shift to cloud-based security tools.
* Many organizations will benefit significantly from utilizing the hybrid infrastructure that helps you use your existing investments and begin to realize the value of Zero Trust initiatives more quickly.
* Fortunately, each step forward will make a difference in reducing risk and returning trust in the entirety of your digital estate.
* We provided a few leading ZTA maturity models including the one we've developed in partnership of Deakin University in Australia. This facilitates an opportunity for organizations and security leadership to consider adopting the right one or customizing a new maturity model with relevant components that fits your specific needs.

Zero Trust should be the key security strategy for all companies, and implementing it requires unified analysis and enforcement across all users, devices, resources, and environments that eliminate siloes and blind spots to accurately assess the context of each authentication and enforce adaptive access policies everywhere.

Hed Kovez, CEO and Co-Founder, Silverfort

Chapter 4

Identity Is the New Security Control Plane

4.1 Why Identities and Why Now?

In today's modern environment, our online identity, is incredibly important to us, whether it's logging into your favorite social network to connect with other people across the world; accessing applications to work from your devices at home; or increasingly, for essential government services. In constructing and confirming these identities, we lean on trusted institutions – organizations such as governments, banks, and major technology companies. They are the keepers of our digital identities, confirming we are who we say we are. We must trust them to protect our data when we set up an account, and every time a security breach occurs, it damages that trust. In the modern digital world, digital identification is an opportunity and a necessity for many individuals and organizations to access services and participate in the modern economy.

The importance of digital identity is a concern in a world where almost one billion people today lack legally recognized forms of identification. Of the more than six and a half billion people who do have some form of identification, at least half cannot effectively use that ID in today's digital ecosystem. This conveys a massive advantage on individuals who have firm digital identification and is a significant barrier to businesses, governments, and other organizations that seek to conduct online services. Well-designed digital identification or "digital ID" can enable individuals to access vital digital services – education, banking, government benefits, and more. Digital ID is also crucial for an organization's security and userbase knowledge. When verified, Digital ID unlocks opportunities for innovative service provision and user support. You need to ask yourself:

- Has my agency successfully developed trust in our digital transformation?
- Are we prepared for the new security challenges posed by digital transformation?
- How can we protect and use identity in our digital transformation?

Zero Trust security framework talks about being able to verify conditions to establish trust dynamically, for all entities, on a per request basis and

DOI: 10.1201/9781003225096-7

(ideally) continuously throughout the session. As more and more applications of the world start living on the open internet and "connected" devices get embedded in our daily lives, the type of entities that need to be verified to establish basis of trust become varied and distributed. However, one common denominator that connects all these entities is identity.

That's why it's relevant to keep the identity at the center of the transaction.

In the study conducted to identify The Top Security & Risk Management Trends for 2021, Gartner identified that one common priority for many security leaders is to leverage Identity First security (Figure 4.1).

Figure 4.1 Gartner's Summary of Top Priority Security and Risk Trends.

This becomes essentially compelling with the shift to remote working (priority#1 for most employers), which is enabled by leveraging the cloud for infrastructure and services, mobilizing the workforce, and adopting the "work from anywhere" model globally.

Digital transformation forces re-examining traditional security models, as the old way of security does not provide business agility, user experiences, and protections needed for a rapidly evolving digital estate. Many organizations are implementing Zero Trust to alleviate these challenges and enable the new normal of working anywhere, with anyone, at any time.

4.2 Identity – Building Trust in the Digital World

As industries worldwide have started to digitize, from automated manufacturing to mobile banking platforms, the identity platform that supports these functions has been facing increasing challenges verifying who you say you are and what level of access you are authorized for. Due to this strain, attackers are increasingly targeting this potential vulnerability. Therefore, it is essential that all digital identity platforms be secure, usable, and trusted. This applies to everything from using blockchain for social security purposes to long-standing financial institutions.

As we expand digital ecosystems and continue to use increasing amounts of data, new trust issues around security and identity are being raised. As we add more touchpoints where data is collected and exchanged, it also means more potential points of entry and an increasing attack surface for attackers. Your entire business depends on the ability of users to access the services they need in a secure and trustworthy way. If you lose the trust of your customers or if these services aren't available when customers need them, the consequences are severe. It is due to this that verification has become essential – all data and sign-ins need to be treated with skepticism. Trust must be built through verification.

Only when all elements involved can trust in the security of data and communication as well as the protection of their intellectual property can digital enterprises function properly. Developing this trusted relationship will enable different elements to interact via secure identities. It is through this that trust and identity form the cornerstone of successful digital transformation. Without identity modernization and verification, it is nearly impossible to establish the trust necessary for different aspects of the digital enterprise to function properly together. Without trusted and secure identity, the vision of remote, empowered, and efficient workers will not come to fruition.

Let's start by understanding the initial identity architecture in the modern enterprise (Fig 4.2).

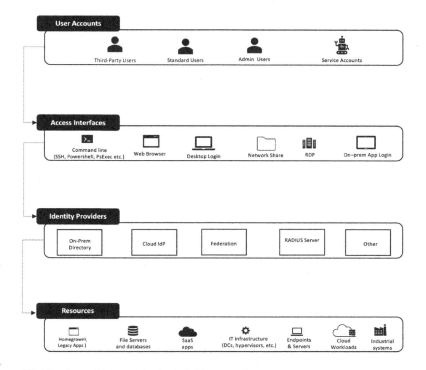

Figure 4.2 Identity architecture in the hybrid enterprise.

Figure 4.2 shows a standardized view of the hybrid enterprise's identity architecture. On top, there are **users** – internal, external, regular, privileged, human, and machine to machine. These users interact with enterprise resources through various **access interfaces** – the main ones are listed in the diagram's second layer. The third layer in the diagram shows the various **identity providers** where the actual authentication takes place. Upon providing the correct credentials, each type of directory enables the users access to their destination resources which can be seen in the last layer.

Identity Zero Trust architecture attempts to implement these pillars in the domain of **authentication** and **access attempt**. This is done by integrating an additional flow – Zero Trust flow – to the third layer in the identity architecture we've shown before, the **identity providers** layer.

As you can see, Figure 4.3 shows the whole process that takes place in the range between where a directory gets an access request and where it grants or blocks access to the requesting users.

The different shading colors represent what we perceive as the four key pillars to implement these principles in practice: **Unification, Context, Enforcement,** and **Granularity**.

These pillars are how the Zero Trust core principles can take actual form in the identity control plane, with each pillar corresponding to one or more principles as shown in Table 4.1. The table shows how these pillars map against the Zero Trust principles.

4.3 Implementation Pillars

Let's explore each of these implementation pillars in more detail.

4.3.1 Unification

Unification is the ability to have 360 real-time visibility into all authentications and access attempts across all on-prem and cloud resources made by human and machine users through any access interface using any authentication protocol.

4.3.1.1 Zero Trust Principle

Unification is the initial prerequisite for sound implementation of the Verify Explicitly principle, since it ensures that all the required data points are made available for reliable risk analysis and anomaly detection.

4.3.1.2 Architecture Placement

Figure 4.4 shows how unification can be achieved. All authentication is performed against the various directories in the hybrid environment. Hence,

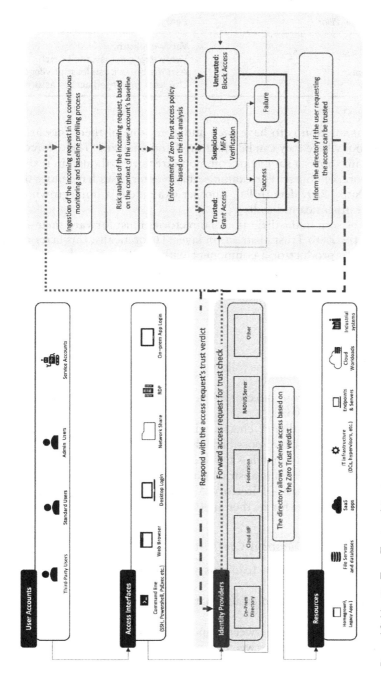

Figure 4.3 Identity Zero Trust architecture.

Table 4.1 Mapping Implementation Pillars to Zero Trust Principles

Implementation Pillar	Zero Trust Core Principle
Unification	Verify explicitly.
Context	Verify explicitly; assume breach.
Enforcement	Assume breach; use least privileged access.
Granularity	Use least privileged access; assume breach.

the logical solution is to have each and every one of them forwarded to a central pool where they can be monitored and analyzed. The colored part in the diagram shows a sample of common directories (though in reality there can be more, of course. For example, many enterprises have more than one cloud Identity Providers (IdPs). Another example is a homegrown application that authenticates locally).

As can be seen in the diagram, all directories must forward their authentication to the Zero Trust abstraction layer. Theoretically, this layer could be a standalone product or a component within one of the directories which is logically separated from this directory's authentication component. However, it should be noted that currently most directories do not natively support such functionality.

4.3.1.3 Flow

The unification flow runs as follows:

- User requests from directory A access to a resource by providing username and password.
- Directory A evaluates checks whether the username and credentials match. There are two possibilities:
- Credentials don't match – Directory A denies access and forwards the data to the Zero Trust abstraction layer.
- Credentials match – Directory A forwards the data to the Zero Trust abstraction layer for further analysis.

4.3.1.4 Actionable Questions Checklist

To evaluate your Zero Trust readiness, you can go over the following checklist:

1. Do I have a single interface that provides real-time visibility into all authentications?
2. Can I easily discern between standard users and privileged users?
3. Can I easily discern between human users and service accounts?

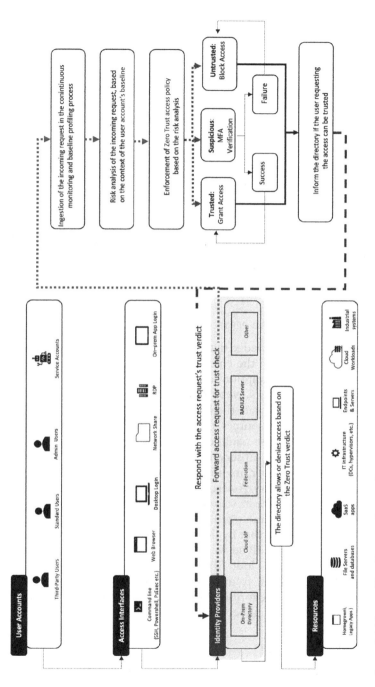

Figure 4.4 Identity Zero Trust: unification focus.

4.3.1.5 Additional Focus Points and Considerations

4.3.1.5.1 END-TO-END

Digital transformation advances in full gear with more and more organizations moving both infrastructure and applications to the cloud. While the productivity advantages are clear, this shift creates significant fragmentation the identity management that bears direct security implications.

Let's consider a standard enterprise environment. It would typically include an on-prem directory (e.g., Active Directory), cloud directory for software as a service (SaaS) applications and infrastructure as a service (IaaS) workload distributed among public cloud of several providers. In addition, there is also a VPN or some alternative for secure remote connection and maybe a solution to secure privileged accounts.

The first step for identity Zero Trust is to ensure that visibility of all authentication and access is available. This entails overcoming the fragmentation challenge to attain a single interface from which one can ensure that there is no blind spot and that every user attempting to access an enterprise resource – whether it is a SaaS application, remote VPN connection, or an on-prem file server – is visible.

4.3.1.5.2 WEB AND NON-WEB PERSPECTIVES

It is imperative to acknowledge that the root cause of the fragmentation challenge is not derived from the enterprise's stage in its cloud transformation journey as the naïve assumption might suggest. The story is not of on-prem vs. cloud but of non-web vs. web resources. Let's illustrate this point further.

When identity is the issue, the key distinction between resources should be made on how these resources are accessed rather than where they reside. For example, an enterprise might consider itself as 100% cloud native, with all SaaS applications and all servers and workload in Amazon Web Services (AWS) or Azure. However, its applications are accessed through the web browser, utilizing Security Assertion Markup Language (SAML) OpenID Connect, and so on, while its servers (though cloud based) are still accessed with Windows New Technology LAN Manager (NTLM) and Kerberos.

In practice, this means that by design, the access to these resources cannot be managed by a single IdP, so we have the fragmentation still at large even when the environment is cloud-born.

The bottom line is that fragmentation of the identity stack is a starting point currently and in the foreseeable future. This is a factor that all identity Zero Trust initiatives should consider.

4.3.1.5.3 SERVICE ACCOUNTS

So far, we've discussed identity Zero Trust and the fragmentation challenge in the context of **resources**. However, an equally important part of the equation are the enterprise users, including internal employees, third-party vendors, and service accounts. The unification pillar requires visibility into every type of user that accesses a resource, regardless of which group this user belongs to.

As a rule of thumb (though exceptions always occur), while this is a rather straightforward process for standard users, it can be more challenging for third-party access, and the biggest challenge resides with gaining visibility and monitoring of service accounts.

A short recap: service accounts are accounts that are not associated with any human user but are used for machine-to-machine communications. While some are created manually by administrators to streamline operations, many are created automatically at the course of new software installation. A common use of service account is in distributing software updates across machines in the environment.

Typically, these accounts are created with high access privileges so they can access other machines and perform the task for which they exist.

The standard information technology (IT) team has neither full visibility to the number of service accounts in its environment nor knowledge of their activity.

This blind spot, in conjoint with these accounts' access privileges, makes them a lucrative target for attackers. It is therefore essential to have full insight into the enterprise's service accounts for all types of identity Zero Trust implementations.

4.3.2 Context

The ability to continuously create a behavioral baseline profile for every user account, based on its entire authentication activity across all enterprise resources, enables reliable and high-precision risk analysis for every new access attempt to determine whether a given user can be trusted to access a resource or not.

4.3.2.1 Zero Trust Principle

The Context implementation pillar complements the Unification pillar in fulfilling the Verify Explicitly principle, being accountable for anomaly detection. In parallel, it is also tightly related to the Assume Breach principle as well, through the risk analysis and threat detection capabilities it delivers.

4.3.2.2 Architecture Placement

The shaded components in Diagram 4.5 show where the Context pillar takes place. The ingestion, aggregation, and analysis of all users' authentications and access attempts across all enterprise resources are the first tasks the Zero Trust abstraction layer performs on top of the continuous data the directories forward.

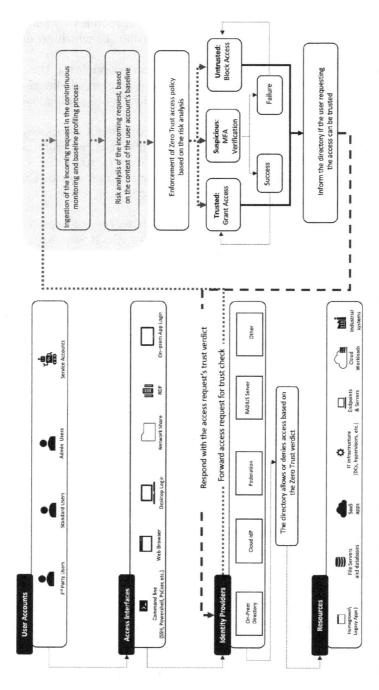

Diagram 4.5 Identity Zero Trust architecture: context focus.

The user's behavioral baseline is derived from as many data points as possible, including but not limited to its individual and group patterns, time, geolocation, type and frequency of resource access and others. In addition to the anomalies, there are other factors that contribute to a user's risk score. For example, repeatedly denied multi-factor authentication (MFA) can indicate that the user's credentials are compromised. Another example is the detection of authentication traffic patterns that are known to be associated with malicious activity such as Pass-the-Ticket, Pass-the-Hash, and others. Each of these examples would elevate the user's risk score.

4.3.2.3 Flow

There are two complementing flows in the Context pillar:

4.3.2.3.1 BEHAVIORAL BASELINE FLOW (LEARNING PHASE)

- Directories forward authentication requests to the Zero Trust abstraction layer.
- Each authentication request is joined to its respective user.
- The authentication request is analyzed to its components (source directory, time, geo, frequency, etc.).
- All components are joined by purpose-built algorithm to compound the user's behavioral baseline.

4.3.2.3.2 SINGLE AUTHENTICATION FLOW

- Directory A forwards an authentication of User X to the Zero Trust abstraction layer.
- The authentication request is analyzed against user X behavioral baseline, the device's risk, and all other related contextual details and is either:
- Normal – User X's risk score stays the same.
- Anomalous – User X's risk score is elevated.

4.3.2.4 Actionable Questions Checklist

To evaluate your Zero Trust readiness, you can go over the following checklist:

- Do I have a risk engine that can ingest all authentication data?
- Can my risk engine determine reliably whether a given authentication is legitimate or malicious?

4.3.2.5 Additional Focus Points and Considerations

While the **Unification** pillar ensured that all the authentication data is available leaving no blind spots of user activity, the **Context** pillar ensures that this data is analyzed to reveal the relative risk of every authentication and access attempt. This is achieved with the following steps.

4.3.2.5.1 COMPLETE AUTHENTICATION TRAIL

Users access multiple types of resources. The first step is to leverage the Unification pillar we've described earlier to reliably associate all authentications and access attempts to the user that performs them. In this manner, the data points that required can be taken for further analysis .

4.3.2.5.2 BEHAVIORAL PROFILE

360-degree visibility into the user's authentication trail enables us to establish a behavioral profile that is based on the user's access patterns across all resources in the hybrid enterprise – shared folders, IaaS workloads, SaaS applications, and any others. The more resources added to the pool, the more accurate the behavioral baseline becomes. In an identity-based attack scenario, the attacker is bound to deviate from the compromised user's standard behavior patterns. In alignment with the Granularity pillar, it ensures that a risk analysis based on this profile would take place upon each new access attempt to increase the number of potential points of failure to the attacker. At the end of the day, the attacker is not the user it has compromised, and a high-precision insight into this user's activity should discern between what's normal and what's not.

4.3.2.5.3 UNIFIED RISK ANALYSIS

A single risk score for each user account is the exclusive reference point, regardless of what resource this user attempts to access. Consider the following scenario: an attacker has compromised an endpoint, gained access to a user's credentials, and performed a Pass-the-Ticket attack to access additional machines. In addition, it also attempts to log in to Office 365 with this user account. Assuming that the Unification pillar is implemented, we're able know that this is the same user.

Since it performed a clearly malicious act in the on-prem environment, we can determine that this user account is at risk not for on-prem resources but for every resource in the enterprise environment. The ability to imply from a risky act on prem to a seemingly normal access attempt in the SaaS environment (or the other way around) is imperative to successfully counter attacks that traverse through the hybrid environment taking advantage of the silos between different Identity and Access Management (IAM) in the identity stack. Having a single risk score that that is impacted from anomaly in accessing resource from type A enables to detect risk when the same user attempts to access resource form type B even if this access attempt seems by itself completely normal.

4.3.3 Enforcement

Enforcement is the ability to trigger secure access controls such as MFA or block access with an access policy across every type of user, access interface, or resource in order to prevent in real time any malicious activity that attempts to utilize compromised credentials to access targeted resources.

4.3.3.1 Zero Trust Principle

The Enforcement pillar is the initial implementation of the Use Least Privileged Access principle since it deals with crafting and enforcing access policies to secure resources and the data they host. In parallel, it is also tightly related to the Assume Breach principle because it also strives to reduce the exposed attack surface to bare minimum.

4.3.3.2 Architecture Placement

Diagram 4.6 shows how both the directories and the Zero Trust abstraction layer integrate to enforce secure access controls upon detecting a risky authentication regardless of user, access interface, and user type. The shaded component on the right represents the access policy that can independently determine whether to allow access, deny access, or require MFA verification, with the MFA verification taking place against the Zero Trust abstraction layer itself. Once a verdict is reached, it is forwarded to the directory, leveraging its native capability to allow or block access.

The Enforcement pillar makes it clear why the directories are imperative to the Zero Trust implementation. This is because they are the only component within the identity stack that has the power to allow or deny users' access to resources in real time.

4.3.3.3 Flow

1. The access request is checked against its respective policy.
2. Based on the policy, the user is approved, denied, or prompted with MFA.
3. The final verdict is forwarded to the directory.
4. The directory acts based on the verdict to either allow or deny access to the user.

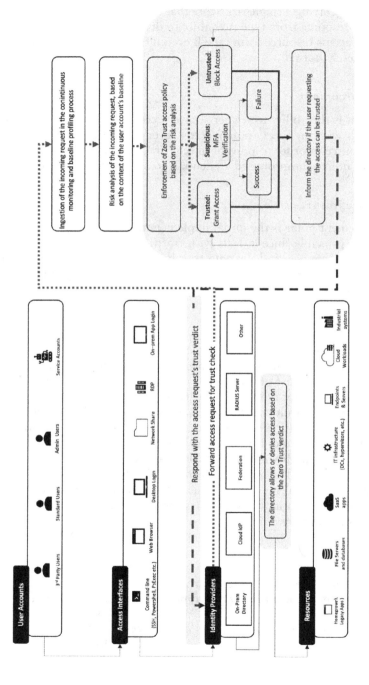

Figure 4.6 Identity Zero Trust architecture: enforcement focus.

4.3.3.4 Actionable Questions Checklist

1. Can I enforce adaptive access policies across all my resources?
2. Can I apply MFA to all my resources and access interfaces?
3. Do I have the ability to block malicious authentications in real time?

4.3.3.5 Additional Focus Points and Considerations

4.3.3.5.1 COMPLETE ENVIRONMENT COVERAGE

Needless to say, the enforcement capabilities must span the entire environment. Anything shorter than this would prevent the Zero Trust implementation from its security value. Consider, for example, the following (and common) scenario: a sensitive file server has an agent that enforces MFA protection on Remote Desktop Protocol (RDP) connections and desktop logins. However, remote access via command line (PsExec, PowerShell, WMI, etc.) is not subject to this protection leaving this server exposed to lateral movement attacks from any threat actor that gained access to compromised credentials.

4.3.3.5.2 ACCESS POLICIES ZOOM-IN

Enforcement takes place in the form of access policies that grant or deny access based on various conditions. This can be achieved either by the IdPs themselves or by an abstraction layer that integrates with them and can act as the decision maker on whether a user is eligible to access a resource or not. This way or another, what's imperative is to have the ability to intercept authentications in real time and prevent non-trusted ones from taking place.

Crafting access policies for Zero Trust implementation entails analysis of the various ways an authentication can be flagged as malicious and hence untrusted. In other words, in order to operate under the Assume Breach principles, one must know what type of authentication can indicate that a breach had indeed occurred. To achieve this, three types of access policies can be conjointly used:

4.3.3.5.3 RULE-BASED POLICIES

These policies pre-anticipate **what an attacker is likely to do,** based on common sense and accumulated knowledge from prior attacks. For example, attackers typically hunt for admin credentials that would render them vast access privileges. A rule-based policy would anticipate that and will allow remote connection with admin credentials only from the admin's machine itself. Any other option would be considered untrusted and will either prompt the admin user with MFA or block access.

4.3.3.5.4 PATTERN-BASED POLICIES

These policies rely on the Context pillar capability to detect in a deterministic manner authentication traffic patterns that are exclusively associated with malicious techniques such as Pass the Hash, Pass the Ticket, Kerberoasting, and others. A pattern-based policy is triggered upon detection of such patterns and can either block access or require MFA verification.

4.3.3.5.5 RISK-BASED POLICIES

These policies are triggered when an access attempt's risk score exceeds a certain threshold the user is not trusted to access any resource. The elevation of the risk score can be either detected during an attempted authentication or rely on prior ones. We can classify risk elevation's root cause to the following types:

- **Failure to authenticate against a rule-based policy.** An example is if a user provides valid credentials yet fails the MFA challenge. In this case, the user is regarded as compromised and its risk score would rise respectively, taking effect for any resource access.
- **Performance of a known malicious pattern.** Here, the level of the risk would match the detected malicious behavior. For example, an attempted brute-force attack indicates that the attacker has obtained just the username, while a Pass the Hash indicates a more severe risk where the attacker has compromised both the username and his credentials (in the form of NTLM hash). We also include in this group any risk data that is received from other security products (Security Information and Event Management [SIEM], Security Orchestration, Automation and Response [SOAR], Endpoint Detection and Response [EDR], etc.).
- **Performance of anomalous behavior the attacker is likely to perform.** In this case, the risk is elevated due to a detected anomaly in the user's behavior based on the user's behavioral baseline (as was described in detail in the Context pillar). Examples are logging in to a SaaS application simultaneously from two different locations, accessing a large number of servers in less than 10 seconds, etc.

4.3.4 Granularity

Granularity is the ability to apply the entire Zero Trust flow upon each individual resource access, enforcing the user to regain trust with every new access attempt, and never assuming that prior access suffices to regard the user as trusted.

4.3.4.1 Zero Trust Principle

The Granularity implementation pillar is tightly related to both Use Least Privileged Access, as well as Assume Breach since it materially increases resilience by creating a defense-in-depth-layer that comprises multiple points of failure.

4.3.4.2 Architecture Placement

Diagram 4.7 shows the entire Zero Trust architecture, since the Granularity pillar is about applying the complete Zero Trust cycle for every resource access attempt.

4.3.4.3 Flow

1 User X requests access to resource A.
2 The full Zero Trust process is triggered. The user is either:

    2.1 Trusted
    2.2 Untrusted

3 User X logs out of resource A.
4 User X's status reverts to untrusted.
5 User X attempts to access resource A again.
6 The full Zero Trust process is triggered again.
7 And so on and so forth for every other resource.

4.3.4.4 Actionable Questions Checklist

Can I enforce a Zero Trust verification process at the level of the individual resource?

4.3.4.5 Additional Focus Points and Considerations

4.3.4.5.1 RESOURCE VS. NETWORK SEGMENT

The Granularity pillar ensures the security check where the user gains trust is placed at the level of the single resource rather than the network segment. Let's break it down to better understand the concept.

4.3.4.5.2 FROM SEGMENT TO RESOURCE

While the most elementary unit in a network based Zero Trust is a network micro-segment, identity Zero Trust can go deeper than this by enforcing users to gain trust upon accessing each individual resource. These result in

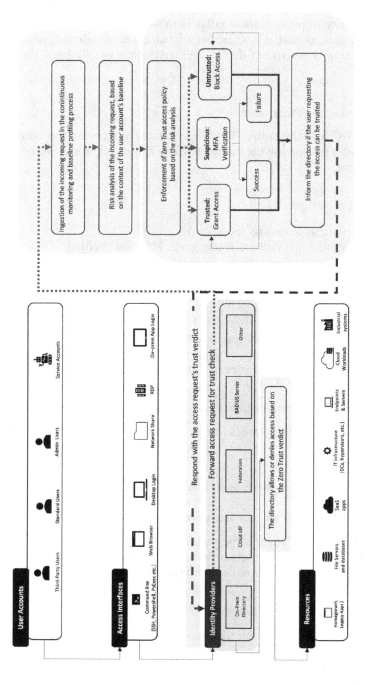

Diagram 4.7 Identity Zero Trust architecture: granularity focus.

material reduction of the attack surface since it significantly increases the points of failure in case of actual attack. To better understand the added value, let's consider the difference between two scenarios – compromise of the network segment gateway renders the attacker potential access to all the resources within that segment, while the compromise of resource access would confine the attacker to the limits of this resource alone.

4.3.4.5.3 FROM RESOURCE TO ACCESS ATTEMPT

This already minimized attack surface can be further reduced by enforcing users to regain trust not only at the initial resource access but also in all further access attempts within it. In this manner, the fact that user A was granted access to a sensitive file server at 1:00 PM doesn't exempt him or her from going through an additional security check when accessing it again one hour later. This creates a multilayered security fabric that can maintain high resilience to identity-based attacks. Even if the attack succeeds at a certain point, it will still have to regain trust over and over again, increasing the likelihood of its detection and containment before inflicting actual harm.

4.3.4.5.4 RECAP OF THE ASSUME BREACH COMPONENT

The Assume Breach component manifests a pragmatic and extremely efficient approach – since we can never be 100% sure that our security controls were not bypassed, let's go all way in the different direction and build our security practices as if we're 100% sure that they are. Translating it into identity terms means that whenever a user performs an authentication to access a resource, we act as if what happens is an attacker impersonating the true user by utilizing the user's compromised credentials.

So, the most logical thing to do is to perform an additional security check before trusting the user with the right to access the resource. However, this cannot stop here because we cannot be that naïve to presume that our security check cannot be bypassed as well! At first glance, it might seem like a dead-end – how can you protect when you assume that your protections are bypassed?

Now we can understand why the Granularity pillar is essential for effective implementation of the Assume Breach principle. While we cannot know for sure that the security check succeeded in fending off threat actors, we can ensure that if it is indeed bypassed, the gain for the attacker will be minimal. In a worst-case scenario, the attacker gets access to a single resource for a limited timeframe.

4.4 Priorities for Modernizing Identity

As we use an increasing number of devices to log in and access data, the simple expediencies of seeing an individual log into their device on premises and of building a security perimeter around your on-premise devices are no longer viable. Industry leaders from all verticals are digitizing essential functions within enterprise to improve competitiveness, gain efficiency, or provide better services to customers. These cloud-enabled digital transformations all create more opportunity for workers to work remotely from their laptops, smartphones, tablets, and other devices. When we enable a modern enterprise with the digital tools and agility needed to work from anywhere, anytime, we need to have a single identity for each employee. This creates an environment where trusted identity is crucial to successful digital transformation and where a simple and secure sign-in process is essential.

Zero Trust is a multifaceted journey that can span many years. Clearly defining the goals, outcomes, and architecture makes organizations more successful than a reactive approach.

The overall approach for evolving identity security involves consolidating all-access paths through a central control plane and then leveraging an intelligent policy engine to ensure only known safe requests get through. The consolidation process ensures that all related entities (users, devices, and apps) integrate with a common identity plane that integrates with a rich set of signals to evaluate and action authentication requests. It should be noted that in this context, the term *identity* just doesn't refer to people identities and incorporates device and application and service (or virtual machine) identities (Figure 4.8).

The policy engine derives its intelligence from multiple sources, including the IdP, user behavior signals, application risk indicators, and device signals.

The Zero Trust approach for identity will take you in the direction of the four priorities discussed next. Through the course of rest of this chapter, we will discuss how to architect an identity platform to achieve these priorities.

When deciding the goals for your identity management, think about how much attention to give to each of these priorities and find the right balance that works for your organization.

4.4.1 Priority 1: Unify Identity Management

Modern IDaaS platforms enable organizations to manage all their identities in a central location, whether they're in the cloud or on premises. The

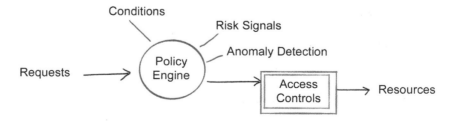

Figure 4.8 Zero Trust access control

key is to think beyond the employee identity and put the IdP in center of all authentication requests. Here are some suggestions to get you started.

- Identity for users – employees, external users such as partners and vendors, and customers
- Apps and identity created for app instances (e.g., service principles)
- Devices – registering devices against assigned users to provide a seamless user experience

4.4.1.1 Control 1.1: Enable Single Sign-On

The wave of identity transformation starts from the unification and simplification of user experience, which involves implementing single sign-on and passwordless experiences across applications.

Most organizations are currently in a hybrid setup from an identity standpoint with their traditional identity from the on-prem directory synchronizing with the cloud Identity Provider (IDP). The latter provides the primary authentication (Figure 4.9).

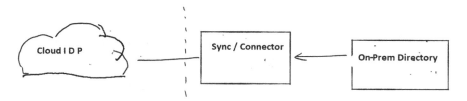

Figure 4.9 Identity synchronization flow

Synchronizing cloud and on-prem directories enables SSO to some core enterprise workloads such as O365, GSuite, Customer Relationship Management (CRM) systems, etc.

Applications with their own identity source give rise to silos of authentication sources and keeps organizations from getting full visibility to authentication risk-taking insightful actions – but more on this later. So, when planning for SSO, it is imperative to look at all other applications and connect to the central identity provider across SaaS apps, on-premises apps, and custom-built apps.

Certain directories, such as Azure AD, natively support SSO for the OpenID Connect (OIDC) and SAML-based applications. For legacy applications that support Kerberos, header-based sign-on, or custom forms-based login, application proxies can negotiate Kerberos token or simply relay the password to enable SSO.

For any other apps that are not covered by these methods, or they are already bring provisioned via a remote access solution, leverage the available integrations to connect them to the common identity stack. For example,

Azure AD integrates with native Microsoft solutions such as RDS and major third-party solutions from vendors such as Citrix, Akamai, F5, Netskope, ZScalar, etc (Figure 4.10).

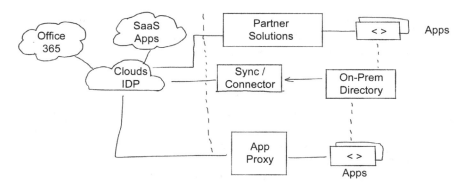

Figure 4.10 Azure AD integration with third party solutions

4.4.1.2 Control 1.2: External Identities

According to Microsoft research powered by Pulse in February 2020, 98% of executives agreed that deepening engagement with customers and business partners is the way to go for the future. Business leaders need to empower all collaborative partners – including distributors, suppliers, vendors, and others – with secure and seamless access to the resources they need while protecting their organization's assets. Additionally, business partners have unique "lifecycles" in their interactions with the organization. Subsidiaries that are constant partners may require longer-term access to resources, in contrast to seasonal or part-time contractors.

To foster real collaboration with partners, it is essential to look at integrating them in the identity lifecycle practices, allow them to securely use their own identity when possible, and provide seamless sign-up and sign-in process. Modern identity platforms enable this while maintaining a low-risk profile, protecting apps and data, and respecting privacy risks for external users and compliance with required standards (e.g., General Data Protection Regulation [GDPR]).

IDP platforms can simplify integration of employee, customer, and partner identity on a common identity platform and encapsulate that with an over-arching layer of identity protection and regulatory compliance.

4.4.1.3 Control 1.3: Enable Passwordless Approach When Possible

Passwords were in use long before computers were invented. Arguably, the Roman military used secret words to distinguish friend from foe. This possibly motivated Fernando Corbató, widely regarded as the godfather of the modern computer password, to introduce password to enable secure time sharing of mainframe computers at Massachusetts Institute of Technology in 1960. The practice has carried on to every system or application created since then.

However, passwords carry the same risks now, as they did in Roman times:

- They are only good as one's memory. Easy passwords are easily guessable, and hard ones are forgotten, and hence people tend to write them down in insecure places.
- If every system demands a separate password, people will reuse some of their passwords.
- If you ask people to change passwords very often, they will follow an easily guessable pattern of change.

Passwordless authentication combines multiple factors tied to the user that replaces the need to provide passwords, making the authentication process secure and seamless user experience.

The process generally involves enrolling the creating trust indicators for a device that the user will primarily use. The sign-in process then confirms the rightful ownership and presence of the established user when providing access.

There are a few IDP platforms now that support passwordless authentication capabilities.

4.4.1.4 Control 1.4: Automatic Provisioning

If applications must maintain their own users separately, there are still options to master the identities in one central place. Many modern apps support System for Cross-domain Identity Management (SCIM) connectors to automate the provisioning of user identities. Another part of user provisioning is making sure users have the right access in connected applications for correct authorization, and SCIM also helps provision the right group memberships to enable appropriate authorization. SCIM was born out of the desire to manage user identities in cloud-based applications and services.

Provisioning identities using SCIM helps implement a controlled identity lifecycle and limits disparity in user provisioning.

4.4.1.5 Control 1.5: Device Integration

Managing the user's laptop or computer helps track these devices with a unique ID and provides access to device indicators that help make better decisions. For example, it makes sense to allow access to data when the user is coming from a managed trusted device but to practice stricter access controls for uses accessing from an unknown device.

Enrolling devices with the integrated identity platform enable benefits such as:

- Seamless SSO from the managed devices
- Using device indicators as an additional signal for the policy engine
- Centralized management of devices for remote monitoring

Onboarding devices provide another layer of intelligence to your Zero Trust architecture for decision making.

4.4.1.6 Control 1.6: Managed Identities

Service accounts create a big attack surface because in most cases, these accounts (1) run with high privilege, (2) hardly get their passwords recycled, and (3) difficult to front with a strong authentication factor.

When possible, it is recommended to leverage modern means of providing access to your sensitive resources. Today, Privilege Access Management (PAM) is a well-documented and mature process, and these practices which encompass service accounts must be built into any Zero Trust model or implementation.

4.4.2 Priority 2: Implement Secure Adaptive Access

4.4.2.1 Control 2.1: Secure Adaptive Authentication

Password is an evil that is no longer necessary. Even if it's not possible to entirely remove passwords from identity, there is a ton of technology available to prevent the need for the user to enter it multiple times. We discussed SSO and passwordless sign-in in the previous section.

MFA helps upgrade that on multiple fronts.

- It helps strengthen the identification process by ensuring the user is who they claim to be.
- It helps make the authentication process seamless by leveraging what I would term "dual-factor" authentication; that is, a secure second factor (e.g., an authentication app or bio-metric scan) encapsulates the password. In addition to providing a passwordless experience, it also prevents passwords from traveling over the line, making the whole process more secure.

Keeping in the spirit of the Zero Trust mindset, the authentication process can be made even stronger by leveraging other authentication indicators to evaluate the request and apply appropriate access controls.

Some of the common indicators that can help decide based on rich context are:

- **Who** – authority and risk of identity (e.g., the presence of strong MFA)
- **How** – device, risk of device identity, browser or application type
- **What** – sensitivity of the content being used
- **Where** – location, changes in location, pattern of usage
- **When** – date time of access, frequency of access

Enriching authentication with such context helps make secure decisions and provides post-access intelligence for investigation if needed.

Modern authentication protocols such as OIDC use access tokens to provide access to required resource. These tokens have a limited lifetime to ensure the compromised sessions have set expiration. If the context becomes stale, the authentication server gets the ability to update the claims and limit access if needed. The authentication servers use this event as an opportunity to enforce MFA or access controls if the new conditions demand so.

OIDC specification announced updated specs for Continuous Access Evaluation (CAE) in August 2019. CAE allows the cooperating Transmitters (apps) and Receivers (authentication servers) to leverage Shared Signals and Events Framework and monitor the validity of access on a more regular basis. Transmitters may send continuous updates using these events, which Receivers can modify access and enforce required access controls.

This is done to ensure:

Conditional access:

- Coverage – dashboard and templates
- Granularity and grouping – filter for devices (for exceptions)
- Grouping – filter for apps
- Authentication method policies

As an example, Azure AD leverages its policy engine called Conditional Access, which integrates with set conditions, risk indicators, and other threat intelligence to decide for individual authentication requests. Similarly, Netskope uses a component of its Cloud Exchange, Cloud Risk Exchange (CRE), to apply conditional access via automated tickets and workflows.

Risk policy engines will become more encompassing and richer, and it is anticipated these will include:

- Improved coverage with conditional access dashboard and availability or ready templates to create policies for common scenarios
- Increased granularity with filters based on specific device properties

- Ability to group policies for multiple apps by using app filters
- Ability to target policies to specific authentication methods

4.4.2.2 Control 2.2: Block Legacy Authentication

Early authentication protocols (now called legacy) were designed with two-party authentication cycle in mind. In such protocols, the application (called Client) interacts with the authentication server to negotiate a token on behalf of the user. There are multiple risks in this process:

- User passes username and password to the application, which then uses that to negotiate access. If the application does not handle passwords or secrets safely, the user becomes at risk.
- As the user is not involved in the negotiation process directly, it becomes difficult to enforce further authentication factors to verify the identity of the requestor.
- Most legacy protocols lack security controls to prevent token replay/hash reuse attacks.

Modern authentication protocols such as OIDC and SAML are designed to overcome these risks. It uses three-party authentication, which means the user negotiates the access tokens directly with the authentication server and then passes them to the application. The obvious benefits include:

- Ability to enforce MFA during a negotiation
- Credentials stay safe between user and authentication server
- Means to leverage parameters that signify client ownership (such as session and nonce) to protect against token replay attacks

When possible, modern authentication protocols should be leveraged, and the use of authentication protocols should be blocked or limited. In many cases, the need of legacy authentication is limited to appliances such as print servers. Prioritize the implementation of policies to limit the use of legacy authentication to these devices using identity-, location-, and service-based restrictions.

In many cases, applications such as Exchange Online provide capabilities to deny legacy authentication requests at the Client level before it reaches the authentication server (Azure AD). When more granular control is required to restrict legacy authentication, you can leverage conditional access to do it based on multiple indicators.

4.4.2.3 Control 2.3: Protect Against Consent Phishing

OIDC standard defines applications and resource servers (such as APIs) as separate entities. This model allows publishing services based on open standards and allows all compatible applications to request access to resources. The request for such resources often appears as a consent form that informs and warns the user about the level of access the said application is requesting and asks the user to approve for the access to be granted.

While the model is instrumental in helping the applications integrate, it can be weaponized and used as an attack vector. An attacker can create a trustworthy-looking app or inject illicit code into a trusted website and use it to phish sensitive details from a user. The website tries to trick an end-user into granting the application consent to access their data such as contact information, email, or documents.

Such attacks are impervious to normal remediation such as password changes or MFA as the access to the identity is granted at this step.

In 2020, the SANS Institute fell victim to a similar attack which resulted in the creation of email forwarding rules, allowing the forwarding of emails to an external email address.

Some actions that can help protect against such attacks include

- Harden the app consent process, including ensuring that no one can grant consent on behalf of the whole organization.
- Monitor access provided to any external apps for risk indicators and employ tools that help you take urgent action to block such apps.
- Look for Indicator of Compromise (IOC) that indicate OIDC attack has taken place and make it part of your Security Operation Center (SOC) rhythm.

4.4.2.4 Control 2.4: Equal Focus on On-Prem Identity

Although many organizations are in a hybrid state for their identities, the on-premises identity server (Active Directory in most cases) seems to be the forgotten entity for ongoing monitoring. Some recent attacks such as Solar-Winds leveraged this gap in SOC visibility to traverse through the organization and infect their development pipeline with malicious code.

It is recommended to include on-premises identity monitoring as part of your identity-strengthening process and to enable SOC to detect advanced attacks in hybrid environments by monitoring user and entity behavior. The solution involves identifying and investigating suspicious user activities and combining with other user indicators to separate benign activities from potentially malicious tasks such as reconnaissance or pass-the-hash attacks. Several security vendors support user and entity behavior anomaly detection that integrates into the broader security ecosystem.

4.4.3 Priority 3: Identity and Access Governance

Proper governance is an imperative part of the identity and access management process. At a broad level, governance can be divided in two streams:

- **Identity governance** – which involves identifying user personas, defining identity ownership, and implementing managed identity lifecycle (joiner, mover, leaver)
- **Access governance** – creating policies to control the user membership and ensure right authorization. In many cases, this is achieved by ensuring use of managed permission systems (such as role-based access control [RBAC]), automatic permission assignment and rollback, and just-in-time (JIT) permission provisioning.

According to Crowd Research Partners, 90% of organizations feel vulnerable to insider attacks. The main enabling risk factors include too many users with excessive access privileges (37%), an increasing number of devices with access to sensitive data (36%), and the increasing complexity of IT (35%).

The identity governance process should be able to help identify the following:

- Who has access to what resources? Who should have access?
- What are they doing with this access?
- Is access over-provisioned for any user? Has there been scope creep due to role or department changes?
- How can we showcase that the access governance controls are working?

The identity and access lifecycle management help manage a user's access throughout their lifecycle in the organization, including:

- Creating identity based on the onboarding of employee entity in the Human Capital Management (HCM) (Human Resource [HR] system)
- Tracking the identity progress for all changes and ensuring that the user only has access to the resources required for their role at any given time. For example, a user may join as a vendor or move to be a contractor, a permanent employee, or manager.
- Deprovisioning the identity when the user leaves the organization

4.4.3.1 Control 3.1: Automate Provisioning and De-Provisioning

Manually keeping a user's state change can easily get out of hand in big organizations. When possible, employ automation to integrate with the HR system to trigger creation or archival of identity based on employee state change. This will help make onboarding and offboarding seamless and ensure that users only maintain access if needed. In addition, these events can be used to assess other risky events (e.g., a disgruntled employee trying to exfiltrate sensitive content shortly before leaving the organization).

Many IDPs integrate with many popular SaaS-based HCM systems to automate the identity lifecycle. There are generally also APIs available to integrate with on-premises HR systems when needed.

4.4.3.2 Control 3.2: Access Lifecycle Management and Separation of Duties

One of the key principles of IAM is maintaining separation of duties, that is, ensuring that all sensitive operations have their function divided between two or more roles and each role has its responsibilities clearly defined. Completing sensitive operations would need these multiple roles to cooperate and reduce the chances of malicious actions.

When implementing access lifecycle management, a role definition should also describe the level of access that role will need to different resources. This will enable the creation of access groups that provide all required access for a role, according to separation of responsibility built into their roles.

The required access group(s) should be assigned when moving between roles, and all unnecessary access groups should be removed.

Proper access management should automate the access request, approval, and recertification process to ensure that the right people have the right access and maintain a trail of why users in the organization the access have they have. Leveraging a modular access control system (e.g., RBAC) will help keep assignments easy to manage.

Entitlement Management helps define access models that consolidate all access required for a specific role. In also enables kicking off custom workflow to integrate access for any external solutions not natively integrated into the Entitlement Management solution.

4.4.3.3 Control 3.3: Follow the Least Privilege Principle

Let's start by defining *privileged access*. In a modern organization, privileged access is administrative access and other application or function-specific roles that can change the way your mission critical apps run and handle data, such as application owner, build manager, etc.

The creation of access groups as discussed above also aids in keeping privileges to required level. Implement a similar request-approval process for all privileged roles that enables JIT provisioning of privileged permissions and tracking all such uplifts.

The traditional process of user access review and privileged access review is still pertinent in ensuring that any gaps in permissions are quickly caught and remediated. When possible, implement solutions to assess over-provisioned permissions and modify access groups to align with required "active" permissions.

Several solutions exist that help organizations instrument Entitlement Management and Access Review capabilities and help implement these processes, aligning with some of the best practices listed here.

4.4.4 Priority 4: Integrate and Monitor

4.4.4.1 Control 4.1: Log and Operationalize Identity Monitoring

With identity playing a central role in the security landscape, it is important to retain logs and monitor user activities from an identity perspective. Every major identity platform provides a comprehensive set of logs to track sign-ins, audit events, and risk intelligence. These logs help us:

- Understand how your apps and services are used.
- Detect potential risks affecting the health of the environment.
- Troubleshoot issues preventing users from getting their work done.
- Gain insights by seeing audit events of changes to the directory.

Ideally, your SOC solution stack should allow you to enrich these logs with signals from your application, endpoint, and network monitoring solutions. Mining these logs can help detect patterns that may uncover identity breach attempts or malicious insider activity.

Furthermore, these logs can also help showcase regulatory compliance and act as alerting mechanism for any suspicious detections.

The logs from multiple systems can be consolidated in the SIEM system, which then becomes the hub for the SOC team to monitor and investigate the enterprise for any potential risks.

This helps SOC teams to detect, prioritize, and triage potential attacks. Rich telemetry from multiple sources is beneficial in eliminating false positives so that the team can focus on real attacks. Furthermore, many SIEM systems also provide SOAR capabilities that are very useful in automating response to known common threats, hence reducing noise and alert fatigue.

4.4.4.2 Control 4.2: Integrate Identity for Auto Detection and Response

Consolidating security logs in a SIEM system is a traditionally common way to monitor and investigate across multiple systems. Many modern security platforms also provide the ability to natively interconnect multiple security solutions to pass intelligence, trigger investigation, and automate coordinate responses. Such native integrations help detections to cross over solutions domains and allow correlation of alerts from multiple sources.

When possible, look for opportunities to integrate security solutions to reap the benefits of cross-domain intelligence.

According to a study by the Ponemon Institute, security teams spend approximately 25% of their time chasing false positives. The same study also highlighted that a big portion of this time is spent investigating incidents to look for actionable insights, building incident timelines, and taking repeatable response actions.

These tasks can be automated using modern security solutions that can pre-correlate and examine attack indicators, filter out insights for investigation, and even take response actions that very closely mimic SOC teams' activities. Leveraging such tools can save precious time which can be spent on actual attacks worth manual investigation.

Automated threat response reduces costs and risks by reducing criminals' time to embed themselves into your environment.

4.5 Chapter Summary

In summary, Identity is a core part of an organization's security posture and plays a role in helping interconnect all other security solutions. By adequately planning identity security, you can employ a Zero Trust architecture that helps ensure:

- Today's security strategy needs a central strong point – identity as the control plane and new perimeter which attackers must overcome. This is how identity becomes the trust boundary: it controls how users access applications and information and from which device. A strongly protected single identity is the core of successful security measures for the modern workplace and having a successful identity and access strategy is crucial to maintain trust while enabling productivity in your organization.
- Access to all resources is individually evaluated by a centralized policy engine and is provided after verification (always verify).
- Identity and access lifecycle is managed to ensure right the access to right people (least privilege principle).
- Identity is integrated with the rest of the security stack to provide rich detection and response capability (assume breach).

References

The Top Security & Risk Management Trends for 2021 (gartner.com)
Zero Trust Summary (easysecops.com)
www.welivesecurity.com/2017/05/04/short-history-computer-password/
Zero Trust Deployment Guide for Microsoft Azure Active Directory – Microsoft Security Blog
SCIM: System for Cross-domain Identity Management (simplecloud.info)
https://devblogs.microsoft.com/devops/demystifying-service-principals-managed-identities

https://docs.microsoft.com/en-us/microsoft-365/security/office-365-security/
    detect-and-remediate-illicit-consent-grants?view=o365-worldwide
www.sans.org/blog/sans-data-incident-2020-indicators-of-compromise/
Microsoft Azure Active Directory External Identities
https://openid.net/specs/openid-caep-specification-1_0-ID1.html
Secure your Azure AD identity infrastructure – Azure Active Directory | Microsoft Docs
Plan reports & monitoring deployment – Azure AD | Microsoft Docs
Ponemon Institute Reveals Security Teams Spend Approximately 25 Percent of Their
    Time Chasing False Positives; Response Times – Bloomberg

Gone are the days of deprecated VPN hair pinning and lateral movement issues. Zero Trust (Cloud) architectures have now evolved from a touted "nice to have add-on" to an imperative for BOTH CIOs and CISOs looking to improve both operational resilience and security controls.

Nick McKenzie, CIO & CISO, Bugcrowd

Chapter 5

Zero Trust Architecture Components

5.1 Zero Trust Components Overview

Instead of assuming everything behind the corporate firewall is safe, the Zero Trust model assumes breach and verifies each request as though it originates from an open network. Regardless of where the request originates or what resource it accesses, Zero Trust teaches us to "never trust; always verify". Before granting access, every access request is fully authenticated, authorized, and encrypted. Micro-segmentation and least privileged access principles are applied to minimize lateral movement and excessive privilege abuse. Rich intelligence and analytics are utilized to detect and respond to real-time anomalies (Figure 5.1).

A holistic approach to Zero Trust should extend to your entire digital estate – inclusive of identities, user behavior, endpoints, networks, data, apps, and infrastructure. Zero Trust architecture serves as a comprehensive end-to-end strategy and requires integration across the elements.

The foundation of Zero Trust security is **Identities**. Both human and non-human identities need strong authorization, connecting from either personal or corporate **Endpoints** with compliant devices, together requesting access based on strong policies grounded in Zero Trust principles of explicit verification, least privilege access, and assumed breach. Furthermore, **user (and entity) behavior** is important here, for if an identity is strongly authenticated, the level of confidence will be eroded if the behavior of that identity is suspect.

As a unified policy enforcement, the **Zero Trust policy** intercepts the request, and explicitly verifies signals from all seven foundational elements based on policy configuration and enforces least privileged access. Signals include the role of the user, location, device compliance, data sensitivity, application sensitivity, and much more. In addition to telemetry and state information, the risk assessment from threat protection feeds into the policy engine to automatically respond to threats in real time. Policy is enforced at the time of access and continuously evaluated throughout the session.

Policy Optimization further enhances this policy. Governance and Compliance are critical to a strong Zero Trust implementation. Security

DOI: 10.1201/9781003225096-8

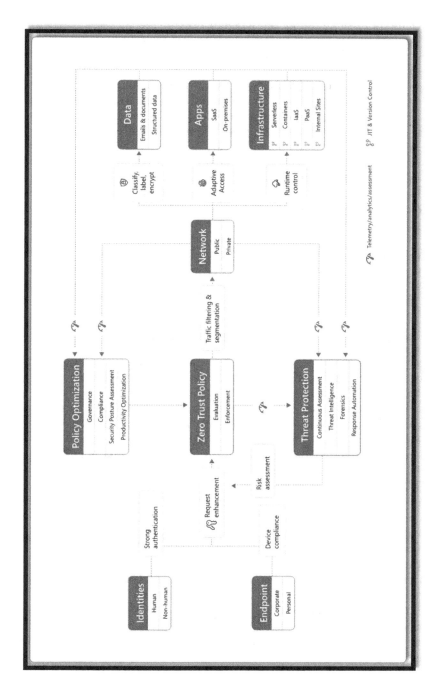

Figure 5.1 Zero Trust architecture overview.

Posture Assessment and Productivity Optimization are necessary to measure the telemetry throughout the services and systems.

The telemetry and analytics feeds into the **Threat Protection** system. Large amounts of telemetry and analytics enriched by threat intelligence generate high-quality risk assessments that can either be manually investigated or automated. Attacks happen at cloud speed – your defense systems must also act at cloud speed, and humans just can't react quickly enough or sift through all the risks. The risk assessment feeds into the policy engine for real-time automated threat protection and additional manual investigation if needed.

Traffic filtering and segmentation are applied to the evaluation and enforcement of the Zero Trust policy before access is granted to any public or private **Network**. **Data** classification, labeling, and encryption should be applied to emails, documents, and structured data. Access to **Apps** should be adaptive, whether software as a service (SaaS) or on premises. Runtime control is applied to **Infrastructure**, with serverless, containers, infrastructure as a service (IaaS), platform as a service (PaaS), and internal sites, with just-in-time and Version Controls actively engaged.

Finally, **telemetry, analytics, and assessment** from the Network, Data, Apps, and Infrastructure are fed back into the Policy Optimization and Threat Protection systems.

5.2 Implementation Approach and Objectives

Enterprises must consider *all* applications when architecting Zero Trust – legacy, non-web applications cannot be "ignored until later." It could be selecting a Zero Trust architecture (ZTA) vendor that supports all ports or protocols. It may include some other intermediary technology like Virtual Desktop Interface (VDI) or virtualizing the application that works in conjunction with ZTA or simply plans to rewrite the application to support modern technologies. Consider needs and differences between cloud-based and hardware-device or hybrid models.

ZTA being based on identity means iterative approaches can be taken when performing infrastructure transformations. Many customers start with piloting ZTA with remote users working alongside Virtual Private Network (VPN); then after user migration, the simply turn off the VPN service.

Similar approaches can be taken when segmenting datacenter networks, especially if an agent-based implementation is used. ZTA projects timed with cloud migrations go especially well together when completed using devsecops frameworks to deploy.

Below is a general plan of attack for a Zero Trust implementation based on the security value and effort to implement (my opinion based on experience).

Depending on available resources and the environment, it could be done sequentially or in parallel.

1   **Protect the users.**

- Endpoint Detection and Response (EDR) to detect endpoint compromise and communicate posture to Identity Provider (IDO) and Policy Enforcement Point (PEP)
- Secure Web Gateway (SWG) to protect against and detect network threats
- IDP Modernization and Password Reduction
- Logging and alert modernization or consolidation

2   **Protect the apps.**

- Segment application access or hide applications from those not entitled to reduce the attack surface.
- Decommission VPN to reduce the attack surface.

5.3 Protect the Data

- DLP to detect and prevent exfiltration
- Cloud Access Security Broker (CASB) to detect and prevent exfiltration
- Isolated Browser Access to prevent exfiltration of sensitive data

4   **Deceive and detect threats.**

- Honeypots and decoys to detect breach

5   **Segment the datacenter.**

- Micro-segmentation of services to help prevent and reduce the blast radius of compromise

5.4 Zero Trust in Multi-Cloud and Hybrid Environments

Developing for Zero Trust using native cloud tools across multi-cloud environments can be an expensive proposition due to all clouds doing it "differently." Selecting a third-party product to perform the ZTA tasks (mainly the PEP or Gateway function) enables standardization and simplicity, effectively creating an overlay architecture to connect diverse cloud environments.

Few enterprises use only web-based apps, so the ZTA architecture design must support legacy or non-web applications.

For many, implementing ZTA is an enabler for business agility and flexibility. Traditional network-perimeter security models are complicated and expensive to install in public cloud environments; therefore, many enterprises today still employ on-premises datacenters for their cloud ingress and egress traffic.

Implementing ZTA negates the need for traditional security stacks, which then opens the door to decommission those datacenters, greatly reducing investment in technology hardware.

Let's look at a case study of a customer who implemented Zero Trust in the hybrid environment using Microsoft and Zscaler technology.

5.4.1 Customer Case Study: Zero Trust in the Hybrid Environment

5.4.1.1 About the Organization

We are a global engineering and construction company that delivers landmark projects for our customers. We serve our clients across a range of markets and international locations and build a better world by applying world-class expertise to solve our clients' greatest challenges.

5.4.1.2 Current Challenges

- **User Performance** – As a global company, cloud adoption was proving to be difficult as all network traffic was being backhauled to our centralized datacenters for inspection. Collaboration with local partners in remote regions was difficult due to the increased latency. Local internet breakout was key to our organization's cloud aspirations and a cloud-based ZTA platform was crucial for securely delivering that capability.
- **Mobility and User Experience** – Consumer apps like Facebook, Netflix, and Amazon on mobile devices have a secure, always-on, frictionless user experience. We always aspired to give our users the same experience with our corporate applications, but it became more difficult as the security landscape changed. To continue offering this same experience, we needed more details about the user and device being used and continual verification of the access. ZTA along with a modern identity provider provided contextual information throughout the application use that traditional access and authentication methods could not offer.
- **Organization Agility** – The information technology (IT) organization was very capital expenditure (capex) heavy, meaning that in difficult economic times, the IT budget could not flex enough with the company as required without affecting services. Adopting cloud-based services with the pay-as-you-go mentality was the enabler for an agile organization that could resize our services as required without affecting operations. Attempts to replicate legacy network perimeter architecture to support a cloud-only organization proved to be too complex and cost prohibitive. Saying no to cloud was not an option, and to move forward, we had to change our security strategy to one incorporating Zero Trust.

Technology Solutions

The constant theme throughout the solution was "always on": Access, Security, and Education.

• ZSCALER

Zscaler internet access provides security that enables direct internet access. Our users now have the same security posture whether they are in the office or a coffee shop without the option to turn it off. It is also the secure transport for SaaS applications, with DLP and CASB capabilities.

Zscaler Private Access (ZPA) provides always-on, contextualized access to corporate applications. By abstracting the application access away from the network, we can limit application visibility to only those who are entitled to use the applications and reduce the scope of lateral movement and malware infection if an endpoint gets compromised. Posture controls allowed us to ensure a machine was not compromised before granting access to applications. ZPA was also the key component that allowed us to place applications in *any cloud* and realistically consider closing datacenters.

• MICROSOFT AZURE ACTIVE DIRECTORY

Azure AD is the Identity Provider that we partnered with Zscaler to offer secure, frictionless, always-on access through conditional access and passwordless technologies. Our users had full access to their applications just by looking at the cameras on their corporately managed devices.

• AZURE AND OFFICE 365

Office 365 and Azure became the first-choice landscapes for our applications – Office 365 for collaboration-type apps and Azure for IaaS-hosted servers and PaaS developed applications. Combined with Zscaler, we were no longer restricted to our centralized datacenters for hosting applications, and we could stand up new cloud-hosted locations in minutes through automation.

Policy Changes and User Education – Previously, IT security teams tried to operate unseen in the background to secure the enterprise, but the new technologies allowed us to change strategies, and we started to actively warn users if potential risky activity was detected, like visiting sites that Zscaler had not categorized or were newly created or if they were downloading potentially unsafe files. We also started piloting managed-device only access for some sensitive applications, replacing the blanket bring your own device (BYOD) attitude from the previous decade with contextualized access policies.

5.4.1.3 Top Three Challenges Faced While Implementing New Zero Trust Architecture

1 **Changing mindsets**

Contemplating an architecture change from a centralized model in which *every* packet is captured and stored to a decentralized, Zero Trust model initially ruffled quite a few feathers. After a lot of education, evangelism, and testing, the IT security teams became comfortable after proving out the platform. There was no challenge on the user side because the new access method was quicker and easier than before.

2 **Resources**

As ZTA is based on identity, the transformation journey can be performed iteratively without generally affecting current application access. The speed of this transformation is related directly to the number of resources that can be applied to the project, and for many (including us), it will be a multi-year journey. With the number of resources available, we had to balance the need to change with current operations, and it will be a few years until fully complete.

3 **Taking a hybrid approach**

It may ease minds to implement ZTA while retaining old policies and old security operations practices. Often, trying to mix old and new makes the transformation *harder* and can reduce the effectiveness of the changes. IT and security policies can get in the way of ZTA, and the organization must be empowered to review and modify if appropriate.

5.4.1.4 Impact and Benefits Achieved by a Zero Trust Project

- **Business Agility** – is a broad category that captures the following:

  - Enabling secure cloud use without the need for complex or expensive security architecture
  - Rapid deployment of resources without affecting security
  - Cost and capex reduction by removing legacy tech like security stacks, MPLS, and datacenters
  - Cloud + ZTA greatly simplified the IT infrastructure and reduced management overhead

- **Visibility** – Our first steps into Zero Trust was for remote laptop users – after implementation, we had greater visibility into their application traffic than we did for our on-premises, in-office users. The next step was naturally to implement ZTA for office locations.

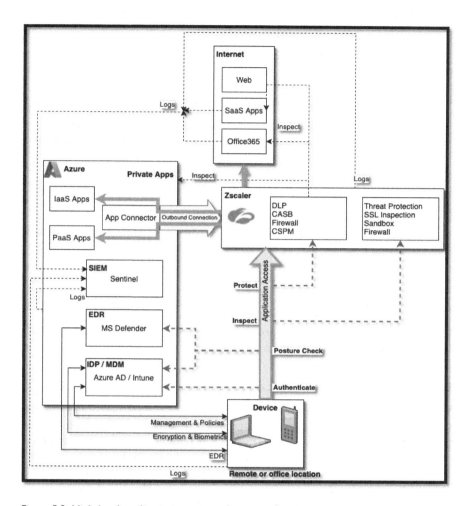

Figure 5.2 High-level application access architecture for the construction company.

- **User Experience** – Implementing ZTA improved user experience across two categories:
  - **Application access** – ZTA with powerful IDP capabilities allowed us to create an always-on, contextualized experience using biometrics for authentication, ensuring only the applications the users were entitled to were made visible to them.
  - **Application performance** – with the rapid push toward the cloud, remote users gained a performance boost using the cloud-based SWG within the ZTA platform, which unlocked more capabilities

for the users that would have otherwise been impossible if their traffic was backhauled to the datacenters (Figure 5.2).

Let's look at the architecture in detail. This architecture has four major themes:

1   Device is managed and protected with encryption, EDR, and biometrics

   a   Access from unmanaged devices depends on the sensitivity level of the data. Some apps may be allowed, some may be blocked, and some may be allowed through other means like isolated browsers and VDI.

2   All application access is:

   a   Authenticated before the app is reachable
   b   Posture checked to ensure device is healthy and compliant before access is given
   c   Inspected to prevent malware
   d   Protected against data exfiltration

3   Public Cloud configuration and SaaS apps are inspected by CSPM and DLP platform components
4   All application access components are logged and sent to central security information and event management.

5.5 Secure Access Service Edge and Zero Trust

Security's origins began in the network. Over time, numerous tools jockeyed for position in data centers and competed for attention from administrators. They were generally effective when applications and data remained on premises and users worked from traditional offices. Some of the tools offered mechanisms to communicate among themselves. But as users moved out of offices and data and applications moved into the cloud, legacy tools became blind. They all operated under one overarching assumption: applications, data, and users are static. Because this assumption is no longer valid, these tools have lost much of their suitability. They don't work with each other, they don't scale well, they lack unified administration, and – crucially – they can't perform their functions when the data are stored and processed on someone else's infrastructure.

Secure Access Service Edge (SASE), an architecture defined by Gartner in 2019, promises to overcome the limitations of too many tools and too many consoles. SASE combines common network functions (e.g., Software-Defined Wide Area Network [SD-WAN], WAN optimization, Quality of Service [QoS], routing, Content Delivery Network [CDN], others) with common security functions (e.g., SWG, CASB, ZTA, VPN, Firewall as-a

Service [FwaaS], Remote Browser Isolation [RBI], others) into a consolidated architecture with unified administration. Policies apply access control to any application or service and monitor and control the movement of sensitive information from and to all users and resources. SASE delivers network and security functions from the cloud, ensuring a consistent user experience wherever users and applications reside.

Good SASE architectures implement Zero Trust principles. SASE consolidates all the way users access resources while remaining neutral to how confidence is assessed and access is granted. Zero trust principles insist that access is granted, and confidence is monitored based on sets of conditions while remaining neutral to any given technical architecture. When combined, SASE and Zero Trust represent a fundamental change to the ways companies protect their digital assets.

SASE can be a reasonable basis for developing an effective Zero Trust program that encompasses fully hybrid environments in which users, applications, and data can be anywhere.

At a high level, and depending on vendor capabilities, companies that adopt a SASE architecture with Zero Trust principles can expect to:

- Gain user risk and application risk insights to determine a level of confidence in the access granted under varying conditions and adapt access based on the confidence factor.
- Extend Zero Trust principles beyond only private applications to web and SaaS applications based on risk insights with adaptive policies and postures.
- Apply risk insights within applications to control access to specific activities (for example, a low-trust scenario that permits viewing and commenting but prohibits sharing and deleting).
- Activate additional security services such as remote browser isolation and advanced data loss prevention based on the assessed level of risk or trust.
- Continuously monitor for changes in context that require a reassessment of trust (e.g., reauthentication, step-up authentication, alteration of permissions, or increased or decreased access).
- Reduce overall attack surface area by eliminating the exposure of protocols and services to the public internet.

Be wary of vendors stitching together legacy technologies and calling them SASE. Combining firewalls, SD-WAN, and VPN only very loosely fits the definition of SASE.

5.5.1 Secure Access Service Edge Architecture Overview

SASE is a flexible security approach that focuses on enabling secure access to resources from anywhere, like Zero Trust, the SASE approach recognizes the

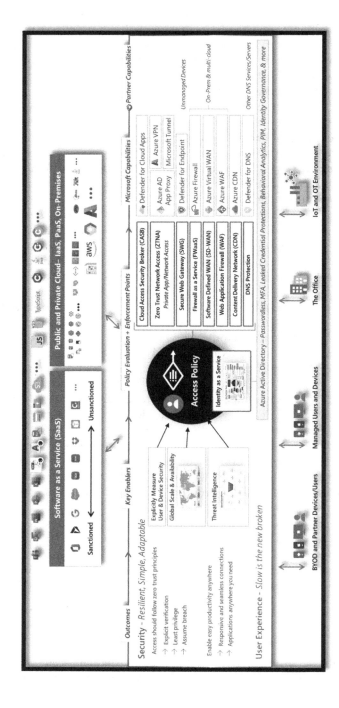

Figure 5.3 Microsoft view of SASE architecture.

business imperative to enable people to securely work anywhere and access to any resource they need (across multiple clouds and on-premises) (Figure 5.3).

SASE Outcomes and Enablers: The key outcomes of a SASE approach are a good **user experience** and strong **security** assurances:

- **User Experience** – SASE recognizes that user experience and performance are critical in this new world where users believe that "slow is the new broken."
- **Security** – SASE also follows the same principles of Zero Trust. Security must design strategies with an assumption of the breach (anything could be compromised), trust must be verified explicitly, and it provides least privileged access using just-in-time and just-enough access using risk-based adaptive policies.

To provide these, the SASE approach requires key enablers, including:

- **Global scale and availability** – to ensure that authorize applications are responsive and perform well for users
- **Explicit measurement user and device security** assurances:
- **Identities** – strong authentication, the account isn't compromised, etc.
- **Device** – compliant configuration, not infected by malware, etc.
- **Threat intelligence** – to inform these security decisions with up-to-date context (drawn from a dataset that is both high volume and highly diverse). This helps quickly filter out known threats and accurately measure risk (avoiding false positives and false negatives that create business risk or interrupt productivity)

5.5.1.1 Policy Evaluation and Enforcement Points

Making SASE real requires using these enablers to *make and enforce access decisions across the diverse set of devices and services* that comprise the "edge" of your modern digital estate.

The organization's **Access Policy** considers these signals in deciding whether to grant, deny, monitor, or restrict access for resource access requests.

The **policy enforcement points** apply this access decision across the estate, ensuring that a consistent policy is applied across SaaS applications, cloud infrastructure, cloud platforms, and on-premises resources.

5.5.1.2 Microsoft Capabilities

Microsoft recognizes that no single vendor today has all the capabilities required for a full SASE solution. Microsoft is focused on ensuring you can have a complete SASE approach with a combination of native cloud capabilities and by working closely with our Microsoft Intelligent Security Association (MISA) partners.

You can implement a large percentage of SASE concepts today with Microsoft capabilities:

- **Identity as a Services – Azure Active Directory (Azure AD)** provides Identity and Access control for all your cloud and on-premises resources, with integrated security that provides strong assurances for employees; partners (Business to Business [B2B]); and customers, clients, and citizens (Business to Consumer [B2C]) across any platform or cloud, including:
  - *Passwordless and MFA* – capabilities to simplify the user experience and strengthen security assurances via *Hello for Business* biometric authentication, *Authenticator App* (works on any modern mobile phone), and *FIDO2 keys*
  - *Identity Protection* – against highly prevalent attacks with Leaked Credential Protections, Behavioral Analytics, Threat Intelligence integration, and more
  - *Azure AD PIM* reduces risk by providing just in time access to privileged accounts using approval workflows.
  - *Identity Governance* helps ensure the right people have access to the right resources.
  - *Azure AD B2B and B2C* provide security for partner and customer/client/citizen accounts while separating them from enterprise user directories.
- **CASB – Microsoft Defender for Cloud Apps (MDCA)** provides CASB capabilities that provide XDR for SaaS applications as well as governance, threat protection, data protection, and more for these SaaS apps and the data stored on them. MDCA integrates with other capabilities in Microsoft's portfolio to extend them to SaaS applications to simplify management and security.
- **Zero Trust Network Access (ZTNA)** – provides **Private App and Network Access** for devices coming from public networks.
- **Azure AD App Proxy** extends the modern access control approach (security perimeter) to on-premises resources by simplifying user access to them and modernizing security with Conditional Access (which explicitly validates user and device trust, a Zero Trust principle).
- **Azure VPN** provides site-to-site and point-to-site VPN access for your resources that aren't yet provided through Azure AD App Proxy. **Azure AD** also provides enhanced security assurances for both Azure AD and any existing VPNs you may have.
- **Microsoft Tunnel** for Microsoft Intune provides a VPN capability tailored to the mobile device experience.
- **SWG – Microsoft Defender for Endpoint (MDE)** provides Web Content Filtering for managed devices as part of endpoint security capabilities.

Microsoft also works with our MISA partners to provide a full SWG capability for managed and unmanaged devices using network traffic interception.

- **Firewall as a Service – Azure Firewall** provides a managed, cloud-based network security service that helps protect resources accessed via Azure networks (including TLS Inspection, IDPS, URL Filtering, and Web Categories). Microsoft integrates with partners that provide this capability for resources accessed via on-premises and on 3rd party cloud networks.
- **Web Application Firewall (WAF) – Azure WAF** provides centralized protection of your web applications from common exploits and vulnerabilities accessed via Azure networks. Microsoft integrates with partners that provide this capability for resources accessed via on-premises and third-party cloud networks.
- **SD-WAN – Azure Virtual WAN** is a networking service that brings many networking, security, and routing functionalities together to provide a single operational interface. This is available in Azure regions around the globe integrates with many partner offerings.
- **CDN – Azure CDN** offers organizations a global solution for rapidly delivering high-bandwidth content to users by caching their content at strategically placed physical nodes across the world.
- **DNS Protection – Microsoft Defender for DNS** protects resources that use the Azure DNS's name resolution capability. Partner solutions can provide additional protection for other name resolution capabilities.

5.5.2 Customer Case Study: Secure Access Service Edge Implementation

About the organization: It is a global Fintech that provides payment services to consumers as well as merchant platforms and finance with approximately 1000 employees.

5.5.2.1 Current Situation and Current Challenges

- User behavior and accountability – Trying to get users out of the "we are a start-up" mentality. Moving to a global company means the company needed to think bigger and have a better security focus.
- Board and executive buy-in – Until a board member (from a different company) was compromised, the company had very little support from the board on any security functions.
- Legacy systems and getting them into the ZTA such as no more intellectual property (IP) whitelisting and so on.
- User education – This was a key issue for the company. Users didn't know what they were doing was "wrong." After this was explained, most users understood and tried to adjust what they did or work with the security team to find a suitable way forward.

5.5.2.2 Technology Solutions Used to Overcome the Challenges

- **Netskope** – The company phased out IP whitelisting office IPs and legacy VPNs, and ensured all possible access to systems, SaaS, IaaS, and so on were through the Netskope platform one way or another. The Netskope platform played a vital role. When IP whitelisting was involved, the company whitelisted the external IP of the publishers to ensure control access was appropriately controlled.
- **NextGen AV** – The company ensured this was rolled out on VM or containers as well as on every machine. This helped add a layer of visibility and protection.
- **CASB** – Originally not Netskope (later phased out and now using Netskope). The company implemented a dedicated CASB and used this to monitor SaaS apps. This allowed the company to understand what staff were doing and help educate users on why things cannot be done. From there, the company ensured that policies began preventing certain scenarios.
- **Multi-cloud**: Microsoft Azure and AWS were used for IaaS and SaaS services (Figure 5.4).

5.5.2.3 Impact and Benefits Achieved

- Visibility – The company did not know anything about the environment or what the users were doing. Once the company saw data flows

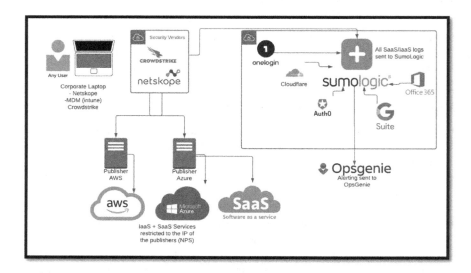

Figure 5.4 High-level implementation overview.

and user behaviors, they were able to implement training, policies, and notifications to help.

- DLP – The company was able to prevent potential data loss constantly and consistently.
- Up time – Visibility also helped to keep a better uptime

5.6 Identity Component

The Identity Service Provider (IDSP) is arguably the most important component of a ZTA environment and must be able to support the needs of the enterprise. Supplying contextual information to the ZTA platform helps make intelligent access decisions. IDSP are maturing rapidly and with Machine Learning (ML) involved are an extremely powerful tool to help securing the enterprise.

When discussing the context, we refer to the Kipling's Method of 5W1H, that is, who, what, when, where, why, and how. Examples include:

- **Who** – ID of the user or service
- **What** – what device is it coming from (e.g., corporate, personal, mobile, CASB). Correlate with history of "what" "who" has logged on before. Is it a healthy endpoint?
- **When** – not just controls based on time of day but is also the time of data access out of character based on ML
- **Where** – geo fenced or network boundary option. Also, is the location or network different than what is expected or out of character?
- **Why** – is the type of data access out of character? Has it happened before (e.g., finance vs. engineering vs. human resources [HR])
- **How** – How did the user or service prove their identity? Just username and password? Is it a cached credential? Was multi-factor authentication (MFA) involved? Biometrics? Take decisions; potentially step up the auth if required.

There are many users within any organization, but no user is the same. They all require a level of access to specific resources, and associated controls must be applied appropriately.

It is crucial to follow full identity lifecycle management, starting with provisioning through management and governance to de-provisioning, when the identity is not needed anymore. De-provisioning is a step when many organizations fail because of a lack of proper process.

A complete ZTA implementation has the user entitlements sourced automatically via the users' roles and attributes contained within the enterprise's Identity and Access Management (IAM) and HR systems. As users leave or change roles, their entitlements are automatically removed. Ad-hoc entitlement requests will always be required, but they should be kept to a minimum with strong attestation processes applied.

Breach avoidance and avoidance of data corruption are primary outcomes derived from good identity governance and access management programs. If the right users have the proper access to the correct data at the right times, the risk of breach and corruption impacting a company's operations, and customers is minimized. Identity governance and access management programs must be able to address the following:

- Access management

  - User profile mapping and access control models
  - Provisioning, deprovisioning, and transfers

- Credential assessment

  - Authentication and authorization
  - Single sign-on and MFA
  - Privilege access

- Governance

  - Access governance
  - Request and approval process
  - Reconciliation and error processes

5.6.1 Identity Architecture Overview

We have provided an overview of implementation of identity architecture in the previous chapter. For this section, we introduce Silverfort (www.silverfort.com) as one of the newest technology players in the identity protection domain.

Silverfort enables MFA, risk-based authentication (RBA), and Zero Trust policies across all sensitive corporate and cloud assets – including systems that couldn't be protected until today – without requiring any agents, proxies, or code changes.

In addition, Silverfort extends protection to interfaces and access tools that currently allow attackers to bypass all other MFA solutions (Remote PowerShell, PsExec, etc.)

Let's look at how Silverfort integrates with Microsoft Azure AD.

5.6.1.1 Silverfort and Azure AD Integrated Identity Zero Trust Solution

The integration between Silverfort and Azure AD enables Azure AD to extend its risk analysis and secure access control to any resource within the hybrid environment. So, Azure AD can provide a complete Zero Trust implementation across the identity control plane.

Azure AD delivers best-of-breed secure access controls to modern web and cloud applications. However, core enterprise resources still don't natively support the authentication protocols Azure AD works with and are hence excluded from its protection. Prominent examples include legacy applications, workstations and servers, IT infrastructure, and many more. In addition, there might be other cloud IDPs that also manage a portion of the enterprise cloud and web applications in large environments.

This means that Azure AD would face significant challenges in implementing the Unification pillar, since there are resources that are out of its scope by design. This is where the integration with Silverfort comes into the play.

Silverfort pioneers the first Unified Identity Protection platform that can deliver identity Zero Trust by integrating with any type of directory within a given environment and executing the Zero Trust flow discussed in the architecture section. As such, Silverfort is uniquely positioned to protect all the resources that natively don't support Azure AD. Moreover, **Silverfort also enables Azure AD to manage them by including them in its identity protection as if they were cloud applications**. By this, Azure AD can secure all the resources in the environment.

High-level insight into this integration is shown in Figure 5.1.

Let's understand how this work in more detail.

5.6.1.2 Unification

Silverfort connects to all the non-Azure AD directories in the environment. These can be Active Directory, federation servers, or other Cloud IdPs. Following the connection, all the directories forward the access requests they receive to Silverfort, awaiting its verdict before granting access. Let's zoom in on what's happening now.

Figure 5.5 Silverfort and Azure AD Zero Trust integration.

5.6.1.3 Silverfort's "Bridging" Capability

Silverfort has developed a unique capability to "bridge" non-web resources to Azure AD, creating for each of them an application object within Azure AD itself. From this point onwards, Azure AD can treat them as if they were standard applications. That means that the Azure AD team can now include them in Azure AD's SSO and configure for these resources access policies within Azure AD that include all of Azure AD's security controls such as Conditional Access and MFA. With this, Silverfort enables Azure AD to fully comply with the Unification pillar's requirements since it now indeed governs all resources within the enterprise's hybrid environment.

It is essential to understand that the bridging capability is the cornerstone of this Zero Trust integration, and the only way Azure AD protection capabilities can be extended across the entire enterprise environment to deliver a truly comprehensive Zero Trust implementation.

5.6.1.4 Context

The Context pillar is enabled by Silverfort' s bridging and executed by Azure AD's risk engine. Due to Silverfort' s bridging, Azure AD can elevate the precision of its risk analysis since the dataset it operates on is no longer limited to cloud and web apps alone but rather includes the entire authentication and access attempts activity across all users, access interfaces, and resources within the hybrid enterprise.

5.6.1.5 Enforcement

The enforcement pillar is conjointly executed by Azure AD and Silverfort. Regarding the cloud and web application, the process is straightforward and carried out by Azure AD policies as before. For the bridged resources, the following flow takes place for each access request:

- Azure AD evaluates whether to trust the requesting user and either grant or deny access based on the respective access policy (which Silverfort' s bridging made possible to configure).
- Azure AD forwards the verdict to Silverfort.
- Silverfort forwards Azure AD's verdict to the relevant directory.
- The directory enforces Azure AD's verdict on the access attempt.

5.6.1.6 Granularity

The Granularity pillar is implemented in Azure AD policy configuration interface. All adjustments regarding the enforcement of the Zero Trust flow are determined and controlled when configuring the access policy (Figure 5.6).

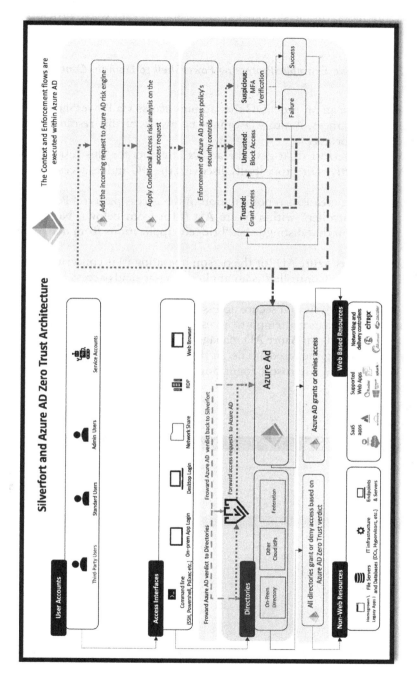

Figure 5.6 Silverfort and Azure Ad's Zero Trust architecture.

Figure 5.7 offers a deeper dive into the joint Silverfort and Azure AD architecture based on the standard architecture diagram we've provided in the former section:

5.6.1.7 Illustrative Example: Protecting PowerShell to Domain Controller Access

Suppose we have an on-prem DC that admins access via PowerShell. Under regular circumstances, Azure AD cannot be aware of this resource's existence, let alone protect it.

However, Silverfort (that gets the access attempts for this resource forwarded from Active Directory itself) discovers the DC and its access method (Figure 5.7).

Silverfort then creates a representation of the access pattern "PowerShell to Domain Controller" within Azure AD (fifth from below). Notice that the Silverfort icon that distinguishes 'bridged' applications from native ones (Figure 5.8).

Again, as far as Azure AD (or the person operating it) is concerned, 'PowerShell to Domain Controller' is an application – it sends access logs, it can be accessed through Azure AD SSO and most important, it is subject to Azure AD risk analysis and secure access controls (Figure 5.9).

From now on, if a user attempts to access the DC via PowerShell, the experience is like accessing an Azure AD managed application (Figure 5.10).

After providing the credentials in PowerShell terminal, the user is prompted with the Microsoft login pop up and further challenged with MFA if needed.

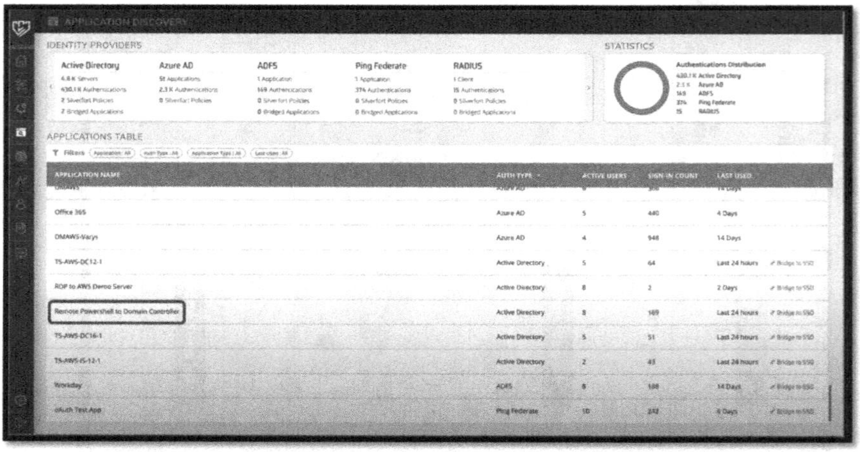

Figure 5.7 Silverfort's Discovery page.

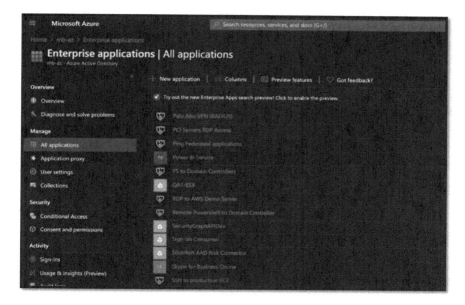

Figure 5.8 Azure AD with Silverfort' s bridged resources

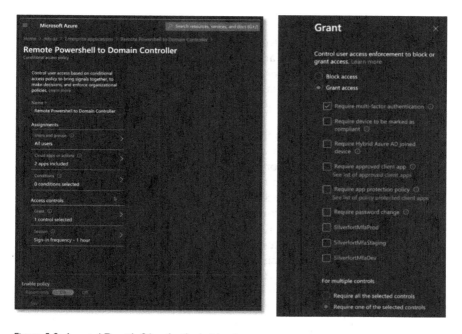

Figure 5.9 Azure AD with Silverfort' s bridged resources.

Figure 5.10 PowerShell to DC Microsoft log-in.

5.6.2 Customer Case Study: Unified Identity Management with Zero Trust

5.6.2.1 About the Organization

This is a Fortune 100 company with a global presence and 100,000 employees.

5.6.2.2 Current Challenges

The main challenge is straightforward – to materially increase the resilience of the enterprise environment against identity-based attacks that include or are based on utilizing compromised credentials to access enterprise resources as is the case in most types of lateral movement.

The following list includes the main inhibitors in reaching this goal:

- Legacy mission-critical applications: These applications are at the core of our business processes and must be protected from compromise. However, these applications cannot be fully covered with standard agent-based MFA, nor can they natively be managed in Azure AD
- Service accounts: lack of sufficient visibility into these accounts, let alone protect them from compromise
- Exposed access interfaces: Remote PowerShell, PSExec, Remote Registry Editor, and other remote access interfaces are extensively used in the environment and must be guarded against a scenario of compromised credentials.
- Siloed IAM: Enrich Azure AD Conditional Access with data from other IAM in the environment to enhance context and accuracy.
- Privilege Access Management (PAM) access: Harden the security of the PAM solution by placing MFA protection on accessing its components.

5.6.2.3 Technology Solutions Used to Overcome Existing Challenges

This was the identity infrastructure and security controls we had to begin with.

- **Directories** – Active Directory and Azure AD and Active Directory Federation Services (ADFS) are where all our users are authenticating to.
- **MFA** – in-house customized Microsoft (MSFT) authenticator.
- **PAM** – Beyond Trust is used to increase security of privileged accounts.

To implement Zero Trust in the identity control plane, we used Silverfort as the backbone and integrated it with our infrastructure in the following manner:

- **Active Directory** – Silverfort is connected to all our DCs enforcing risk analysis and MFA enforcement to all the resources they manage, including servers, workstations, application servers and all other non-web resources.
- **Azure AD** – Silverfort is connected to our Azure AD and thus has full visibility to all SaaS and web-based authentication traffic.
- **ADFS** – Silverfort is connected to our ADFS server, providing full visibility and access control to all our federated applications
- **MFA** – Silverfort solution integrated with the legacy customized MSFT authenticator and make it possible to transition use it in conjunction with Azure MFA (Figure 5.11)

5.6.2.4 Top Three Challenges Faced While Implementing
         New Zero Trust Architecture

- From a risk analysis and context perspective, it also takes some time to establish a reliable behavior baseline for all users to reliable profile what's normal and what is anomalous.
- Discover all the sensitive resources (applications, servers, etc.) as well as all the employees who can and should access them as well as their different privilege level.
- Due to the large scale of the environment, it takes some time to find the optimal blend of access policies that provide the end-to-end coverage this Zero Trust project had set out to achieve.

5.6.2.5 Benefits Achieved by Implementing Zero Trust Architecture

On a high level:

- **Unification** – Access policy (adaptive and rule-based) can now be configured for all cloud and on-prem resources from a single, unified interface.

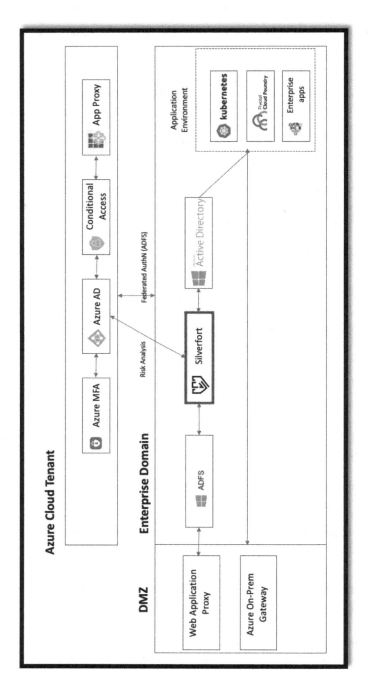

Figure 5.11 Identity Security integration with Azure AD and Silvert solution.

- **Context** – Having all the authentication and access attempt data available for analysis enables a high-precision risk analysis on all users and all resources.
- **Enforcement** – Secure access controls such as MFA and Block Access can now be implemented across all users and all resources.

In terms of the specific challenges listed, all were addressed. The legacy mission-critical applications, service accounts, and access interfaces are all included in the Zero Trust implementation under access policies.

The integration with the directories in the environment ensures that there are no blind spots and that all users and resources are included.

5.7 Endpoint or Devices Component

Times have changed since organizations required "only" company-managed devices. Today, users demand a variety of devices to do their jobs, so many organizations have started to accept BYOD. Having a good asset inventory is essential for a managed set -of company-controlled devices, as they all must be identified, isolated, and secured by implementing policy-based controls. However, businesses must provide secure access to resources beyond just a company-provided device.

There is an increasing need for companies to allow access from third parties, which in turn will result in access from untrusted endpoints, in addition to the previously mentioned BYOD.

An organization must take endpoints (trusted and untrusted or otherwise known as managed and unmanaged) into account when they are defining their Zero Trust access policy. This is not a one-size-fits-all policy, either; hence the need to understand the user and business context.

In some scenarios, unmanaged devices will be afforded the same application (and subsequently data) access, as managed devices. In some cases, they will not; more on this in the section on risk scoring.

5.7.1 Endpoint or Devices Architecture Overview

When implementing Zero Trust for devices, we recommend you focus first on these **initial deployment objectives**:

- **Devices are registered with cloud identity providers.** To monitor security and risk across multiple endpoints used by any one person, you need visibility in all devices and access points where that may be accessing your resources.
- **Access is only granted to cloud-managed and compliant devices and apps.** Set compliance rules to ensure that devices meet minimum security

requirements before access is granted. Also, set remediation rules for noncompliant devices so that people know how to resolve the issue.

- **Data loss prevention (DLP) policies are enforced for BYOD and corporate devices.** Control what the user can do with the data after they have access. For instance, restrict file saving to untrusted locations (such as local disk) or restrict copy–paste sharing with a consumer communication app or chat app to protect data.
- **Endpoint threat detection is used to monitor device risk.** Use a single pane of glass to manage all endpoints in a consistent way and use a SIEM to route endpoint logs and transactions such that you get fewer but actionable alerts
- **Access control is gated on device risk for both corporate and BYODs.** Integrate data from Mobile Threat Defense (MTD) vendors, as an information source for device compliance policies and device conditional access rules. The device risk will then directly influence what resources will be accessible by the end user of that device.

Let's go through two examples of how we have seen customers tackle their Zero Trust journey.

The first is to separate their Zero Trust environment from their corporate environment. This mean using things like App Protection Policies, Defender for endpoint, Intune, Azure Active Directory, and Azure Identity Protection to protect your data in the cloud but allow a small number of extremely locked down devices to stay on corpnet. See Figure 5.12.

An alternative approach is to use ConfigMgr Cloud Management Gateway (CMG) to provide remote users access to on-prem resources without the use of traditional VPN. This is being used by several customers to bring benefits of Zero Trust to the existing workforce while they add new devices and mobile users directly to the Zero Trust environment (Figure 5.13).

Using Log Analytics and Microsoft Sentinel they get the deep visibility into both on-prem and cloud activity to make sure the risk conditions are controlled.

Wherever you are in your Zero Trust cloud management journey – whether you're still thinking about your move to Intune, you've already started with co-management, or you are completely on the cloud – use Microsoft Endpoint Manager. It truly is your hub to unify security, apps, access, compliance, and end-user experience across your entire technology estate.

And because it can leverage Microsoft's powerful data set, it is also intelligent, delivering analytics and signals to keep you ahead of change so you can keep costs down and keep your organization running smoothly, whatever the future brings. And we believe partners are key to success, and Endpoint Manager is also the integration point for the ecosystem.

A few additional points to consider for Zero Trust device architecture are:

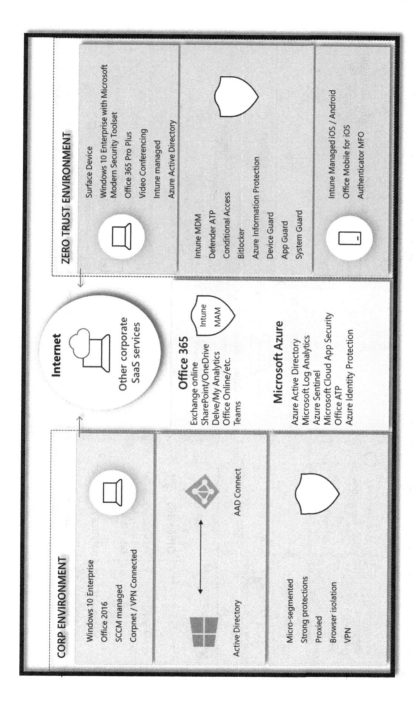

Figure 5.12 Hybrid Endpoint Zero Trust deployment model.

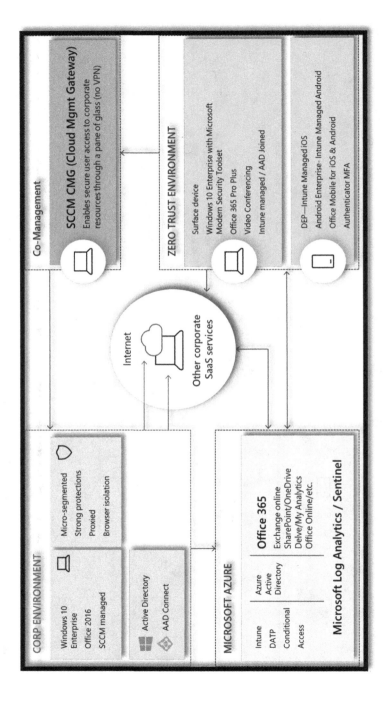

Figure 5.13 Co-managed devices using the Cloud Management Gateway.

- The EDR must be tightly integrated with the ZTA to ensure compromised devices can be denied access quickly.
- End-user devices must be managed for ultimate contextual information, preferably by a cloud-based MDM solution integrated tightly with the IDP.
- Fallback access solutions must be offered when the end-user device does not pass posture controls, whether it is compromised with malware, or a non-managed machine is being used. Application delivery via isolated browsers, access via VDI (where only the pixels are sent to the device) are secure alternatives.
- Move your environment away from passwords and towards FIDO2.0 authentication devices and workflows. Users with managed devices that have FIDO2.0 capabilities built into the device, and OS can go completely passwordless. Those without managed devices should be pushed towards passwordless, multi-factor devices, such as smartphone authenticator apps or physical tokens protected by biometrics.
- Logs from the devices should be forwarded onto a SIEM for collection and alerting wherever possible.
- Out-of-band Digital Forensics and Incident Response (DFIR) capabilities should be considered for suspicious or compromised devices.

5.7.1.1 Customer Case Study: Unified Endpoint or Device Management with Zero Trust

5.7.1.1.1 ABOUT THE ORGANIZATION

A large FinTech organization in multiple office locations.

5.7.1.1.2 CURRENT CHALLENGES

- It started with trying to find a solution for developers to take them off the corporate network and allow the flexibility to install tools in a designated, safe, and accessible environment.
- Subsequently focus shifted to the thinking of next gen standard operating environment (SOE), cloud native not dependent on on-prem tools and services, keeping the environment ever-green and update.
- Make the user experience seamless regardless of where they're working from yet be able to control it more granularly

5.7.1.1.3 TECHNOLOGY SOLUTIONS USED TO OVER THE CHALLENGES

The original project was built around solutions from a couple of vendors, Microsoft being the key one with:

- Device Azure AD joined (not on prem joined) and managed with Intune enforcing number of key policies as part of the base compliance baseline
- Azure AD (AAD) with Conditional Access (CA) at the heart to validate access conditions around user and the device
- Zscaler Private Access to provide granular network access to the internal resources based on user centric policies. ZPA itself is reliant on AAD CA to ensure it can be used only on trusted and compliant devices and by trusted users.
- AAD Passthrough Authentication to provide seamless SSO, including support for Kerberos authentication to internal applications from a non–on-prem-AD joined devices.
- Rather than decluttering the traditional SOE, the company built a new one from scratch with only the base productivity software, single browser, and so on and enabled auto updates on everything.
- To provide additional security all devices using ZIA for secure off net proxy, "Windows Information Protection" Intune enforced policy to enforce differentiation between work and other services and apps to prevent corporate data when handled locally on the device.

5.7.1.1.4 TOP 5 CHALLENGES FACED WHILE IMPLEMENTING NEW ZERO TRUST ARCHITECTURE

- Understanding access requirements to ensure appropriate granular access policies could be defined.
- Ensuring internal systems are modernized to remove dependency on JAVA and FLASH that the company decided to not support on the new build.
- Convincing people they can live with one browser that maybe wouldn't be their first choice.
- Finding alternative approaches to capabilities that were traditionally operating in line of the corporate network (proxy, DLP, secure DNS).

5.7.1.1.5 IMPACT AND BENEFITS ACHIEVED WITH ZERO TRUST ARCHITECTURE

It started slowly and faced quite a few critics, but that didn't last long. Once the word spread, more and more people tired with patchy and slow VPN services were quick to jump on the pilot, which created an army of champions advocating the benefits of this solution on our corporate social media platform.

From then that created a movement and generated momentum and publicity that helped to accelerate focus on improving all the glitches like the compatibility issues with legacy applications.

The company managed to have a workable solution prior to the COVID pandemic. This accelerated the adoption of the solutions when work from home became the new norm, and they had to adapt it to the more traditional SOE with the key components of the original solution like Windows 10 device with compliance policy, AAD CA and ZPA.

At that time, most employees were still on Windows 7, and the VPN solution was crumbling under pressure. The company had people queuing up for hours to upgrade their laptops to Windows 10 to get this experience – they moved to nearly 90% on Windows 10 in a couple of weeks.

Today the company is looking at people coming back to offices with no more blue cables on their desks and the internet being the default network.

5.8 Application Component (on Prem, Legacy, Cloud, Mobile App)

Business and operating models have changed with a proliferation of cloud and SaaS applications and services. One of the essential aspects of security is to lock down access to resources – in this case – applications, to a minimum. Zero Trust becomes extremely powerful here as users no longer need to connect to networks but instead connect to a specific application or service utilizing individual isolated sessions.

All organizations should have a clear understanding of the following from the application agreements:

- Application type
- Hosting model
- Confidentiality, integrity, and availability of the application (derived from the data it accesses, stored, or processed, or business process it supports)
- Transaction flows – upstream and downstream
- Third-party access requirements
- The output of an application risk assessment

When considering new applications, cloud-focused organizations look at application architectures in this order (after considering the app's requirements).

The order below also signifies the level of effort (lowest to highest) required to incorporate Zero Trust concepts:

- SaaS applications
- Developed PaaS hosted applications (including vendor-supplied code or containers)
- IaaS-hosted vendor-supplied applications
- IaaS-hosted self-developed applications

Not to forget the mobile applications, you may have heard of Mobile Application Management, but with Zero Trust, it becomes an even more important piece of the puzzle.

Let's look at a few applications architecture models with Zero Trust.

5.8.1 Application Architecture Overview

Modernizing access to applications is critical to improving user experience and security.

- **Cloud Applications** – Most cloud-native applications directly support Zero Trust access control via Conditional Access (Policy Engine).
  - **Existing applications** – On-premises applications are traditionally accessed via a virtual private network (VPN), which introduces many security risks such as:
    - **Weak authentication** – Many VPNs are configured to use password-only or weaker forms of MFA (which often lack threat intelligence integration).
- **Increased attack surface** – Most VPNs provide full port access to all resources of the network when only an application or two is needed.
- **Maintenance challenges** – Many VPNs are on-premises appliances that must be patched and maintained (vs. a cloud service where the provider does this automatically and quickly) (Figure 5.14).

Organizations are increasingly going "beyond VPN" for application access to mitigate these risks:

- Strengthen authentication – Start with configuring existing VPN to use modern authentication services (addresses weak authentication).
- Publish applications via a cloud service like Azure AD App Proxy to remove the VPN dependency (and eventually retire the VPN from all use).

The VPN is kept available during this period and used as

- Fallback option – for applications that aren't yet published
- Application usage discovery – to provide insight on which applications are used most to prioritize which apps to publish first

There are several ways that you can apply Zero Trust protections to your applications. We have already looked at the benefits of an Identity Provider such as Microsoft Azure AD, Okta, or Ping, as the single entity provider for

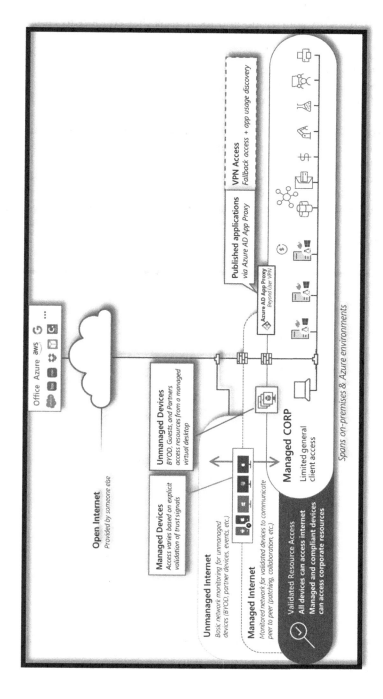

Figure 5.14 Zero Trust Application Access for clients.

authenticated sign-in and the use of conditional access. These recommendations also apply to your cloud and local apps that connect to cloud-based services.

The next strategy to secure your cloud application is by using a Cloud Application Security Broker such as Microsoft CAS, Netskope, or Zscaler CASB solutions (Figure 5.15).

Cloud application security can help your organization with:

- **Discovery** – Use traffic logs to discover and analyze which cloud apps are in use. Manually or automatically upload your firewall and proxy log files for analysis.
- **Sanctioning and un-sanctioning** – Sanction or block apps in your organization using the cloud app catalog.
- **App connectors** – Leverage Application Programming Interfaces (APIs) provided by various cloud app providers to extend protection to Cloud App Security.

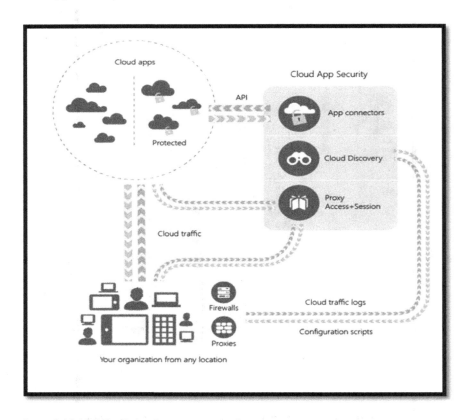

Figure 5.15 High-level cloud app security architecture.

- **Proxy apps** – SAML redirects risky sessions to the reverse proxy to apply app restrictions
- **Data loss prevention** – Prevent data leakage from data transfers from one SaaS application to another SaaS application, and yet again, between instances of the same SaaS application, for example, prevent a user transferring data from a corporate or sanctioned instance of a SaaS application to a personal or non-sanctioned instance of the same SaaS application.

5.9 Data Component

The business is always evolving, but the data lifecycle stays the same. Data is the soul of any business, and it should be treated that way.

While many organizations avoid or find it challenging to do the typical classification of their data, it is imperative to align to the first principle of Zero Trust, "understanding the business context," and complete following steps:

- Understand the data.
  - Discovery (the business must understand the location of data)
  - Classification (the business must define its relative value, then analyze, contextualize, and organize it as such)
  - Map to confidentiality (derived from sensitivity), integrity (derived from sensitivity), and availability (derived from business-critical process).
  - If this is unknown or undetermined, assign these categories (confidentiality, integrity, and availability) to a default rating. These details enable a policy to be applied in the first instance, which can then be further refined over time.
  - Identify data owners and data custodians.

- Protect the data.
  - Inspection (inspect all data, e.g., SSL decrypt)
  - Governance (define rules and guidelines)
  - Control (apply technical control sets)

- Monitor and remediate threats.
  - Monitor sensitive data to detect policy violations and risk users' behavior.
  - Take appropriate actions to revoke access, block users.
  - Continuously refine your protection policies (Figure 5.16).

Many enterprises dream of extensive data catalogues or data lakes, where employees are provided appropriated defined access to data to enable business

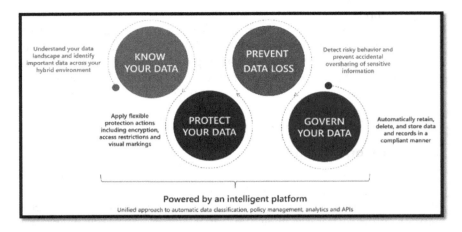

Figure 5.16 Data security lifecycle.

opportunities. These ideals go hand in hand with ZTA concepts, but the data must contain detailed metadata to help determine appropriate access.

5.9.1 Data Architecture Overview

Before embarking on their journey on Zero Trust, most of the organization's data security access is governed by perimeter controls and not based on data sensitivity. Also, the classification and sensitivity labels are typically applied manually.

According to Gartner:

The market for Data loss prevention (DLP) technology includes offerings that provide visibility into data usage and movement across an organization, as well as dynamic enforcement of security policies based on content and context at the time of actions on data. DLP technology seeks to address data-related threats, including the risks of inadvertent or accidental data loss and the exposure of sensitive data, using monitoring, alerting, warning, blocking and other remediation features.

DLP requires discovery and classification. DLP doesn't secure by default. Endpoint DLP typically allows data on the device to remain unsecured while locking down the egress of data off the device.

5.9.1.1 Mobile Application Management

Let's look at the few scenarios with mobile apps. To ensure your data remain safe or contained in a managed app, you need create app protection policies (APPs) in your mobile application management solution such as Intune.

A policy can be a rule that is enforced when the user attempts to access or move "corporate" data or a set of actions that are prohibited or monitored when the user is inside the app (Figure 5.17).

The data protection framework that we encourage you to utilize is organized into three distinct configuration levels, with each level building off the previous level:

- **Enterprise basic data protection** (level 1) ensures that apps are protected with a PIN, is encrypted, and allow selective wipe operations.
- **Enterprise enhanced data protection** (level 2) introduces app protection DLP mechanisms and minimum OS requirements.
- **Enterprise high data protection** (level 3) introduces advanced data protection mechanisms, enhanced PIN configuration, and App Protection Mobile Threat Defense, allowing you to block users from launching a protected app if the device is found to be at risk.

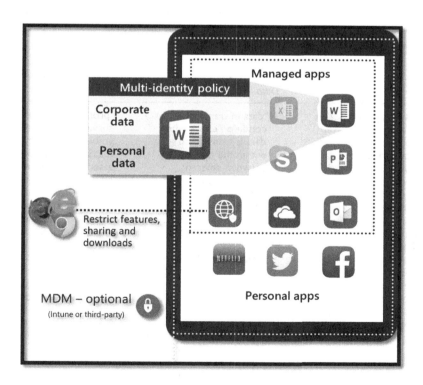

Figure 5.17 Mobile application management.

5.9.1.2 End-to-End Encryption for Data Protection

As part of a comprehensive security posture, data should always be encrypted so that in the event where an attacker is able to intercept customer data, they are unable to decipher usable information.

DLP works by implementing policies set by security or network administrators, which ultimately dictates how data flows out of the network. DLP performs such functions as monitoring access and flow of data, automated classification, alerting, access blocking, anomalous behavior detection, and auditing and reporting.

End-to-end encryption is also applied throughout the following three stages: at rest, in transit, and in use. See Table 5.1 for more detail.

Figure. 5.18 is a visual guide on what kind of information needs to be protected and how to choose the correct encryption type.

Zero Trust is gaining prominence as a viable defense against ransomware and other serious cyber threats. With Zero Trust, an organization can better protect data and be better prepared to recover data and applications without paying a ransom.

Application owners can be confident that their data is safe and that applications will be quickly restored in the event of an attack.

Table 5.1 End to End Encryption

Data at Rest	Data in Transit	Data in Use
Data encryption at rest is a mandatory step toward data privacy, compliance, and data sovereignty. These security services are recommended for this purpose: • Storage Service Encryption • Database Encryption • Secret Management • Key Management • Certificate Management • Hardware Security Modules	A "data in transit" condition exists when data is transferred within the data center between different network elements or data centers. Data in transit should cover two independent encryption mechanisms: • **Application layer** – the HTTPS and TLS encryption that takes place between the client and server node. • **Data link layer** – encryption that takes place on the frames transferred over the ethernet protocol, just above the physical connections	To protect data in use for services across your software-as-a-service (SaaS), platform-as-a-service (PaaS), and infrastructure-as-a-service (IaaS) cloud models, Microsoft offer two important capabilities: • Azure confidential computing • Centralized storage of application secrets AWS offers The Nitro System for confidential computing.

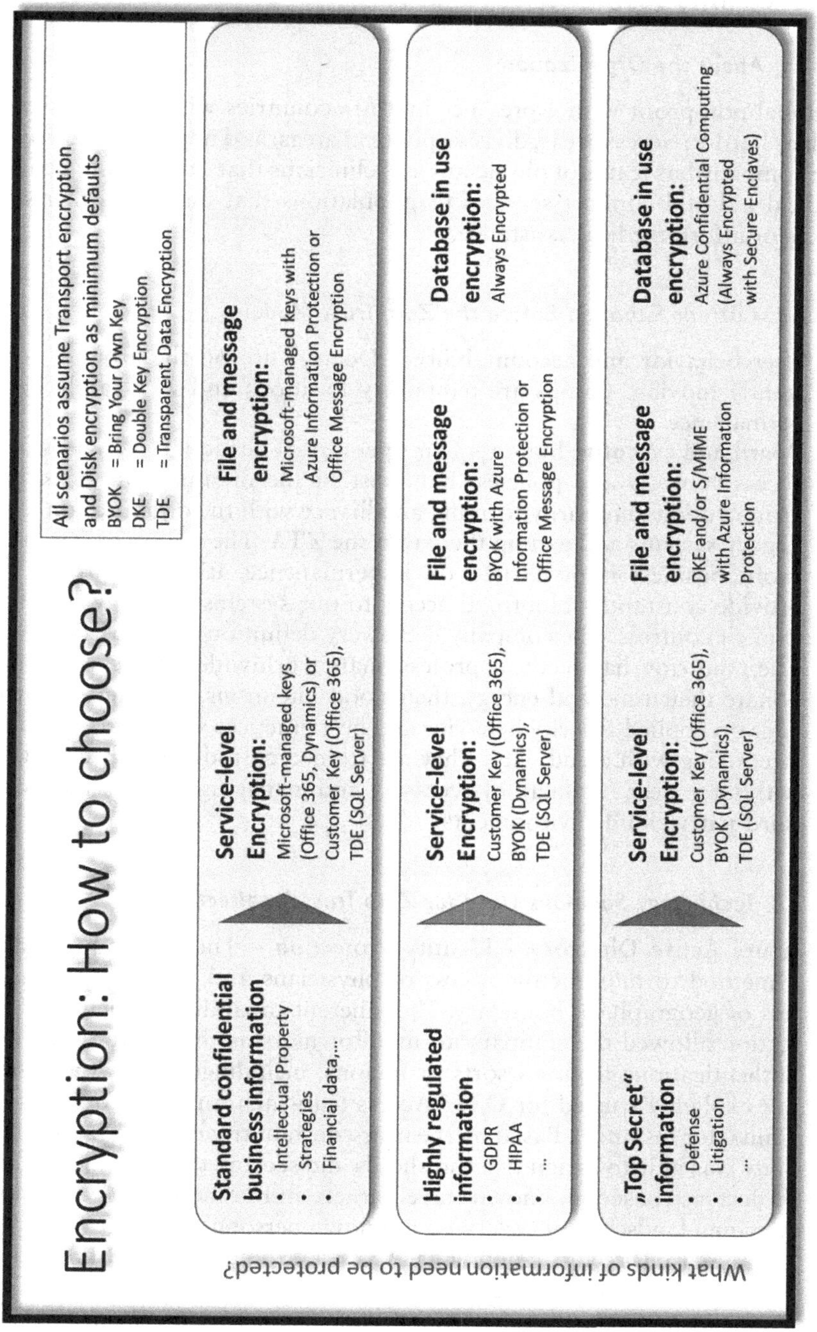

Encryption: How to choose?

All scenarios assume Transport encryption and Disk encryption as minimum defaults

BYOK = Bring Your Own Key
DKE = Double Key Encryption
TDE = Transparent Data Encryption

What kinds of information need to be protected?

Standard confidential business information
- Intellectual Property
- Strategies
- Financial data....

Service-level Encryption:
Microsoft-managed keys (Office 365, Dynamics) or Customer Key (Office 365), TDE (SQL Server)

File and message encryption:
Microsoft-managed keys with Azure Information Protection or Office Message Encryption

Highly regulated information
- GDPR
- HIPAA
- ...

Service-level Encryption:
Customer Key (Office 365), BYOK (Dynamics), TDE (SQL Server)

File and message encryption:
BYOK with Azure Information Protection or Office Message Encryption

Database in use encryption:
Always Encrypted

"Top Secret" information
- Defense
- Litigation
- ...

Service-level Encryption:
Customer Key (Office 365), BYOK (Dynamics), TDE (SQL Server)

File and message encryption:
DKE and/or S/MIME with Azure Information Protection

Database in use encryption:
Azure Confidential Computing (Always Encrypted with Secure Enclaves)

Figure 5.18 Encryption choices

5.9.2 Customer Case Study: Data Loss Prevention and Data Security Zero Trust

5.9.2.1 About the Organization

A global non-profit with a presence in 100+ countries with characteristics such as hard-to-access areas, divisive political areas, and impoverished areas. The company has teams of physicians and clinicians that observe and deliver medical aid and comfort services to populations that may not otherwise access or afford medical assistance.

5.9.2.2 Current Situation Before the Zero Trust Model

- **User behavior and accountability** – Doctors are on the ground, constantly moving. Camps are temporary locations and very rarely have permanence.
- **Board and executive buy-in** – Our operational headquarters have static access controls and policies. But most of the organization is on the ground and temporarily forming an alliance with the organization.
- **Legacy systems and getting them into the ZTA.** The nature of our non-profit business is predicated on impermanence. It's very difficult to provide constantly monitored access to our systems in a way that has explicit controls. The company is the very definition of Zero Trust.
- The company has medical professionals worldwide who periodically donate their time and energy, their good intentions, with zero knowledge on applied security behavior and best practices with managing and interacting with cloud data. They are trained custodians of health data without a clear roadmap of accessing and managing data on the fly in third-party cloud environments.

5.9.2.3 Technology Solutions Used for Zero Trust Architecture

- **Azure Active Directory – Identity Protection** – The company needed a method to monitor the access of physicians and volunteers regardless of geographical boundary. The inherent capability of Identity Protection allowed the company to monitor users as they were triggering authentications from all sorts of regions, including regions that were not explicitly trusted for O365 Access (sub-Saharan Africa or parts of China, for instance). Based on the near-constant travel activity, the company was able to assign risk thresholds and scoring that would increase or decrease based on known travel targets and to monitor a constantly changing landscape of otherwise unknown personnel.
- **Azure Active Directory Conditional Access** – Azure AD Identity Protection policies are one half of the puzzle. Being able to track the geographical

origins of authentication attempts is important. But Conditional Access is the tool that allows the company to gate the access to specific applications and intellectual property. Also, an unsung benefit of Conditional Access is applying Identity and Access Management controls to applications BEYOND the Microsoft Cloud. If an organization has AAD availability in region, they can assign access controls to cloud based applications that support modern authentication measures using SAML or OAuth. This was the difference between success and complete failure in regions not officially sanctioned for the deployment of the O365 tools.

- **Microsoft Cloud App Security** – The tools discussed help ensure that the company has detections and enforcement mechanisms for desired behavior. But MCAS was really the piece that gave a high-level dashboard with the ability to see, across the Microsoft ecosystem, what kind of behavior was occurring from one tool to another. They could see end users traveling from one country to another, easily identifying access hotspots, and identifying when rogue access attempts were present in the environment when compared against the users known travel circuit. Being able to briefly see the access attempts into Outlook, Teams, One Drive, SharePoint, and even third-party SaaS and PaaS applications gave the company real assurance that they were credibility tracking access to sensitive personal and health information databases.

- **User Education** – Conditional Access allowed the company to perform reconnaissance of the environment before putting production-level rules in place. This allowed the company to identify the areas of highest concern, specifically the locations and regions where there was not officially sanctioned support of O365 and Microsoft Cloud. This allowed them to devote extra attention to user messaging campaigns where additional access steps and planning were required.

5.9.3 Top Three Challenges Faced While Implementing New Zero Trust Architecture

- **User Behavior and Accountability** – End users' email, save data, access endpoints, and move from one location to another in nonstandard ways. Creating messaging campaigns to inform staff and volunteers of the new policy was critical to minimize our IT personnel's number of touchpoints. The messaging available from Conditional Access to gently push users in the right decision-making direction was critically important to maintaining availability of our Security Operations staff.

- **Board and Executive Buy-in** – The company's reputation as an internationally available charitable organization of volunteers has the potential to be compromised at any moment by unsanctioned decisions and unmonitored or unprotected behavior from our volunteers and wider userbase. The company leadership had been stuck in an "analysis paralysis" decision making process that had not led to real policy change and outcomes.

- **Legacy systems and getting them into the ZTA.** O365 is not available in *all* the countries of the world. Tenant Creation and the Microsoft Trusted Cloud are not available everywhere.

5.9.4 Impact and Benefits with Zero Trust Architecture

- **Visibility** – Before the Microsoft ZT initiative, the company did not have a clear path to success for being able to monitor our cloud environment alongside our various non-profit headquarters worldwide. Microsoft technologies helped the company create a digital boundary to follow their people.
- **DLP** – Having the ability to monitor and track access to our third-party repositories for data is a game changer. The non-profit pricing available for the higher tier security bundles made it possible for the procurement and SecOps teams to deploy real solutions that protect patient information that is quite literally "on the move."
- **Up Time** – We had near-constant telemetry monitoring and visibility into access attempts across all our users and productivity and collaboration environments. Where O365 was not available, we could bind third-party access controls to our known users and our guest users as they traversed the landscape of non-Microsoft tools.

5.10 Infrastructure Component

Most Zero Trust guidance and standards do not cover "Infrastructure" as a separate component or domain and typically covers this domain broadly under the "Network" component of Zero Trust. However, we want to discuss Infrastructure as a separate domain.

For our context of Zero Trust, Infrastructure refers to all the hardware (physical, virtual, containerized), software (open source, first and third party, PaaS, SaaS), micro-services (functions, APIs), networking infrastructure, facilities, etc, whether on-premises or multi-cloud.

The most important consideration with infrastructure is around configuration management and software updates so that all deployed infrastructure meets your security and policy requirements.

5.10.1 Infrastructure Deployment Objectives

Multi-cloud infrastructures complicate and add cost to an IT organization. This can be reduced by using non–cloud-specific Zero Trust products.

In a multi-cloud or hybrid cloud architecture, consider the following objectives for deployment

- Understand the risk profile and develop a protection plan for it.
- Have the capability to detect and quickly respond to security incidents.
- Enable your security team to have statistical analysis tools for multi-source security incidents.
- Enable your security team to have user behavior analysis tools to detect threats.
- Enable your security team to have emergency response tools to minimize losses from security incidents.
- Use a PAM process that ensures privileged access is only used in a controlled manner.

If we consider Microsoft's cloud, resources such as Azure landing zones, blueprints, and policies ensure that newly deployed infrastructure meets compliance requirements. And Microsoft Defender for Cloud with Log Analytics helps with configuration and software update management for your on-premises, cross-cloud, and cross-platform infrastructure.

5.10.2 Network Component

Legacy perimeter is disappearing, ubiquitous connectivity, and distributed security. It is vital to understand transaction flows and interactions between two or more points. Network isolation and micro-segmentation to more localized segments are some tactics to minimize lateral movement, but they also allow for more granular controls over resource access.

Networking teams already understand the topology, content delivery, and quality of service through performance monitoring and optimization, but Zero Trust introduces more dynamic changes within network architecture where adjustments are necessary.

Endpoints and users do not access networks anymore. Still, they have direct connectivity to an individual service, application, or workload (this is the power of Zero Trust, as we can now shrink our attack surface significantly), so it is crucial to apply the following concepts:

- Adopt the security posture of "Default Deny".
- Avoid "trust zones".
- Use session isolation.
- Use micro-segmentation.

After implementing ZTA, the network outside of the app should only be considered a "canvas" as opposed to a transport mechanism. The only time the network should really matter is for the Zero Trust infrastructure and when components of a service talk to each other without the Zero Trust brokering that traffic, for example, a subnet containing a legacy 3 tier app – ideally that should be isolated, using ZTA or private service endpoints (Azure) or private link (AWS) for inter-app communication.

Consider agent-based micro-segmentation methods over network-based segmentation to simplify implementation. Due to complexity, very few companies ever complete a network-based retrofit on an existing environment.

5.10.3 Network Architecture Overview

One of the recommended approaches for Zero Trust by NIST SP 800–207 is a network-centric approach; the other two approaches are identity centric and cloud-based combined.

The network-centric approach ZTA is based on network micro-segmentation of corporate resources protected by a gateway security component. To implement this approach, the enterprise should use infrastructure devices such as intelligent switches (or routers), Next-Generation Firewalls (NGFW), or Software Defined Networks (SDNs) to act as policy enforcement protecting each resource or group of related resources (Figure 5.19).

A network-centric approach focuses on segmenting the traditional perimeter into sub-zones. Users are considered trusted once inside a zone. While reducing risk to a degree, the network-centric approach is not risk free since it assumes an entity is trusted once inside the zone. For this reason, this approach would require additional security measures and strong identity governance. We have discussed Identity security in our previous chapter in detail.

Following only a network-centric approach has the following limitations:

- It is complex to configure, troubleshoot, and manage, given the multitude of network security zones.
- It introduces a single point of vulnerability: Once users are in the zone, they are free to roam with limited control and visibility on what they do.
- It may not be able to support cloud apps in a trust zone.
- Letting non-employees inside these zones is bad practice but difficult to avoid (e.g., contractors).

5.10.3.1 Segment and Enforce the External Boundaries

With modern architectures and hybrid services spanning on-premises and multiple cloud services, virtual networks – or VNETs – and VPNs – an organization needs to implement several controls, starting with the following.

5.10.3.2 Network Segmentation

Network segmentation is required to limit the blast radius and lateral movements of attacks on your network. No architecture design fits the needs of

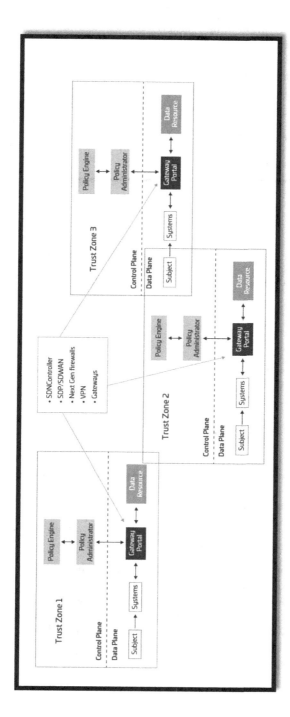

Figure 5.19 National Institute of Standards and Technology network-centric Zero Trust approach.

all organizations. According to the Zero Trust model, you have the option between a few common design patterns for segmenting your network.

There are three common segmentation patterns when it comes to organizing your workload with Cloud Service Provider (Azure, AWS, GCP): Single Virtual Network, Multiple Virtual Networks with peering, and Multiple Virtual Networks in the hub-and-spoke model. Chose the one fits your requirements.

When using cloud service–provided PaaS services (e.g., Azure Storage, Azure Cosmos DB, or Azure Web App), use the private link connectivity option to ensure all data exchanges are over the private IP space and the traffic never leaves the Cloud Service Provider (CSP) network. See Figure 5.20.

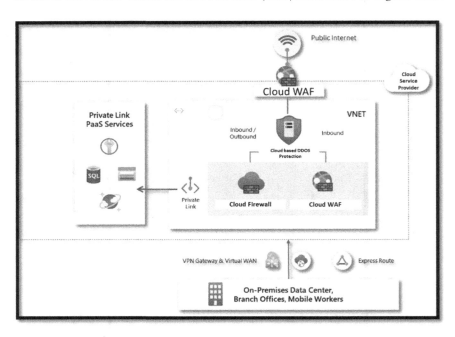

Figure 5.20 PaaS services segmentation.

5.10.3.3 Threat Protection

Threat Protection technologies are meant to harden the network perimeter from malicious attacks such as the distributed denial of service (DDoS) or brute force, and then provide the ability to quickly detect and respond to incidents.

The architecture in Figure 5.21 shows a set of proven practices for running multiple Windows VMs in a scale set behind a load balancer to improve availability and scalability. This architecture can be used for any stateless workload, such as a web server.

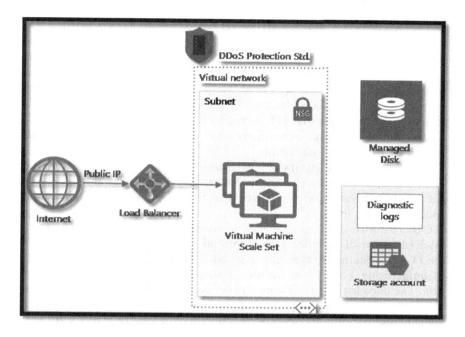

Figure 5.21 DDOS protection with load balancer for multiple VMs.

Virtual machine scale sets allow the number of VMs to be scaled in or out manually or automatically based on predefined rules. The load balancer distributes incoming internet requests to the VM instances. This is important if the resource is under DDoS attack.

5.10.3.4 Encryption

All network traffic, whether internal, inbound, or outbound, needs to be encrypted. This includes encrypting application backend traffic site to site between virtual network using IPsec/IKE policy and encrypting traffic between on-premise and cloud by configuring a site-to-site VPN or configuring IPSec tunnels. A Microsoft detailed guide on this can be found at https:// docs.microsoft.com/en-gb/security/zero-trust/deploy/networks. Other vendor solutions are also available.

Networking represents a great opportunity to make meaningful headway in your Zero Trust journey. Your Zero Trust efforts will not only help your security posture, but most efforts will also help you modernize your environment and improve organizational productivity.

5.11 Zero Trust and Operational Technology Component

Beyond the usual espionage and data-theft attacks aimed at IT systems, threat actors have increasingly turned their attention toward Internet of Things (IoT) devices and operational technology (OT) equipment – everything from oil pipelines to medical devices. Malicious actors have also had success in targeting supply chains, as seen in the insidious Solarwind and Kaseya attacks. This indicates that OT networks have become a primary target of cybercriminals, devising increasingly more sophisticated attacks to disrupt and profit from OT exploitation.

"Fortinet found in its 2020 State of Operational Technology Cybersecurity Report that nine out of 10 OT leaders they surveyed acknowledged at least one intrusion in the past year. 72% experienced three or more".

Cybersecurity is still a challenge to many OT environments due to the modernization of their infrastructure and isolated landscape from rest of the IT. OT systems are typically associated with industry solutions such as manufacturing, energy and utilities, transportation, and building automation. The need for IT or OT convergence for efficient operations and digital transformation requirements have raised the table stakes critical to ensuring safe and continuous operations. This forced industry leader's attention to the concept of Zero Trust as an essential best cybersecurity strategy to modernize the OT infrastructure.

The goal of ZTA is to eliminate all threats, whether they come from outside or within the network. Applying this approach is vital in protecting OT systems, which often must interrogate both network users and a rapidly growing array of enabled Industrial IoT devices. Due to the nature of the devices used in IOT and OT services, there are reduced options to implement ZTA – after all, many of these don't allow you to install an agent that enables Zero Trust on the endpoint. In these cases, Zero Trust gateway-type services should be considered for communication combined with private networks.

5.11.1 A Practical Approach for Deploying Zero Trust for Operational Technology

Securing IoT solutions with a Zero Trust security model starts with non–IoT-specific requirements – specifically ensuring you have implemented the basics to secure identities and their devices and limit their access. These include explicitly verifying users, having visibility into the devices they're bringing on to the network, and being able to make dynamic access decisions using real-time risk detections. This helps limit the potential blast radius of users gaining unauthorized access to IoT services and data in the cloud or on-premises, which can lead to both mass information disclosure (like leaked production data of a factory) and potential elevation of privilege for command and control of cyber-physical systems (like stopping a factory production line).

Once those requirements are met, we can shift our focus to the specific Zero Trust requirements for IoT solutions:

- **Strong identity to authenticate devices.** Register devices, issue renewable credentials, employ password less authentication, and use a hardware root of trust to ensure you can trust its identity before making decisions.
- **Least privileged access to mitigate blast radius.** Implement device and workload access control to limit any potential blast radius from authenticated identities that may have been compromised or running unapproved workloads.
- **Device health to gate access or flag devices for remediation.** Check security configuration, assess for vulnerabilities and insecure passwords, and monitor for active threats and anomalous behavioral alerts to build ongoing risk profiles.
- **Continual updates to keep devices healthy.** Utilize a centralized configuration and compliance management solution and a robust update mechanism to ensure devices are up to date and in a healthy state.
- **Security monitoring and response to detect and respond to emerging threats.** Employ proactive monitoring to rapidly identify unauthorized or compromised devices.

Attackers will choose the 'soft targets' as a point of ingress. Spear phishing or similar attacks allow access to IT systems that can then provide a pathway for attackers to reach OT systems, and the reverse is also possible. In one example, attackers used an aquarium system to access a casino's high-roller databases, demonstrating that any device with connectivity can present a motivated attacker with an opening.

– 2021 Microsoft Digital Defense Report

5.11.2 Internet of Things and Operational Technology Architecture with Zero Trust Principles

The architecture in Figure 5.22 shows how to apply Zero Trust principles to securing OT and industrial IT environment.

This is a sample architecture for Zero Trust deployment for an OT environment with industrial systems. Depending on the industry, it could be logistics, manufacturing, or retail-related industry solutions and systems. There is always an IT environment where the rest of the systems are managed. Ideally, organizations can segment the OT and IT environment by internal isolation, hard boundary, and software boundary for better visibility and control.

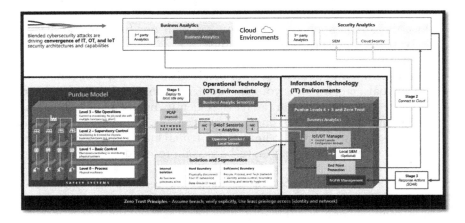

Figure 5.22 Operational Technology (OT) deployment model.

An OT environment requires a sensor to track, monitor, and measure the activity or performance of industrial systems. These sensors are installed in the network (including multiple segments). Once sensors are installed, it can pull data and share it with your site operations or supervisory control systems. If you have installed cloud connected sensors, it can send data to your cloud analytical engine for security governance and threat monitoring purposes. In addition, this information is useful for understanding the environment better – for example, security updates, password management, asset inventory etc.

The IoT or OT manager sits within your IT environment can manage and monitor multiple sensors for tracking and providing better visibility. This information can be shared with local SIEM for proactive threat monitoring.

If you have cloud native sensors, it can send signals to cloud SIEM tool for analysis. Your threat team and SOC team can proactively review the data points and help the management to make informed decision about the security threat related to identity or network exists in your OT environment. You can resonate this approach with your detection and defense in depth strategy and operational protocols.

The endpoint protection can also be deployed to your OT environment. Deployment of endpoint solution would be relatively quicker if the OT systems runs on the IT-supported operating systems (OS). You can also follow a different patching cycle for OT systems to minimize the disruption to industry machines or systems.

There are also business analytical sensors that might be relevant for industry systems in OT environment to measure temperature and vibration. If these sensors are cloud enabled, the data that sensors collect can be sent to cloud analytics for predictive maintenance and operational efficiency.

Last, you can integrate your organization's response action to your OT and IoT cloud analytical engine. This helps the organization to automate response based on the detection of threat and incidents such as malicious email or compromise of identity or compromise devices etc. While attack happening, you can respond through your VPN and lock the user account along the way of conducting detailed investigation.

5.12 Zero Trust and Security Operation Center

The security operations team plays a significant role ensuring an effective Zero Trust strategy, which requires deep visibility and control across organization's infrastructure. Their responsibilities include having visibility into the network traffic, orchestrating data from sources across the infrastructure, applying machine learning for actionable insights, and using automation to respond and take actions. This means that, in practice, the security operations team has plenty to do to monitor and maintain a Zero Trust approach.

One of the significant changes in perspectives that is a hallmark of a Zero Trust security framework is moving away from trust by default toward trust by exception. Zero Trust means that you cannot assume that any of the users, endpoints, credentials, or devices on your network are trustworthy. In a way, endpoints can be compromised, and credentials can be stolen. However, you need some reliable way to establish trust once trust is needed. Since you no longer assume that requests are trustworthy, establishing a means to attest to the trustworthiness of the request is critical to proving its point-in-time trustworthiness. This attestation requires gaining visibility into the activities on and around the request.

Your security operations team must continually monitor for suspicious or anomalous behavior to ensure that everyone is acting legitimately. By deploying an analytics solution that can see across endpoint, cloud and network assets, the team can gain enterprise-wide visibility and safeguard managed and unmanaged assets.

5.12.1 Security Operation Center Automation and Orchestration with Zero Trust

By adopting a Zero Trust approach across identity, network and devices, data, apps, infrastructure, and network, you increase the number of incidents security operation center (SOC) analysts needs to mitigate. With each of these areas generating relevant alerts, you need an integrated capability to manage the resulting influx of data to better defend against threats and validate trust in a transaction. SOC analysts become busier than ever, at a time when there is already a talent shortage. This can lead to chronic alert fatigue and analysts missing critical alerts.

Automation and orchestration bring unparalleled ability to deliver a more efficient and effective security program. With automation, organizations can speed up the identification and resolution of specific threats with a level of precision humans can't compete with. It is all about the right process at the right time.

Many SOC providers offer extended detection and response (xDR) solutions that prevent attacks and detect behavioral anomalies on endpoints and offer holistic visibility, investigation, and remediation capabilities that extend to the network and cloud. SOC often deploys a combination of SIEM and security orchestration, automation, and response (SOAR) technologies to collect, detect, investigate, and respond to threats.

SOC providers also offer SOAR solutions with native threat intelligence capability. The convergence of xDR with SIEM provides an end-to-end picture for an organization to make an informed decision. A well-coordinated Zero Trust principle for SOC is the key success factor to determine the threat vector and remediation capabilities.

5.12.2 Security Operation Center Architecture Components

When it comes to developing a solution blueprint for SOC, a well-known best practice is to avoid selecting best-of-breed components from multiple vendors to build capabilities. Today, many companies offer mature platforms that perform an array of duties that negate the need for multi-vendor complexity. Look for platforms that integrate for other capabilities, such as a ZTA platform that integrates with IDPs using open standards, EDR integration with major vendors, and SIEM integration for log collection (Figure 5.23).

5.13 Defining DevOps in a Zero Trust World

DevOps is a culture that encourages collaborations among all stakeholders, including development and operations teams, and improved processes through automation to increase the quality and speed of software delivery.

Today's security executives who are one of the key "stakeholders" are driving an urgency for Zero Trust model to be designed in and integral to every phase of the software development lifecycle, upgrades, and legacy system replacements. DevOps code persistence, security, and resiliency directly reflect how well ZT principles are integrated with software development life cycle (SDLC).

Adopting Zero Trust into DevOps needs to include specific table stakes or must-have elements if the strategy is going to succeed (Figure 5.24).

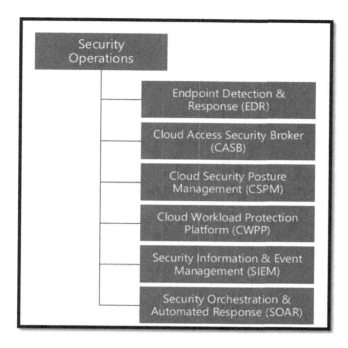

Figure 5.23 Security Operation Center architecture components.

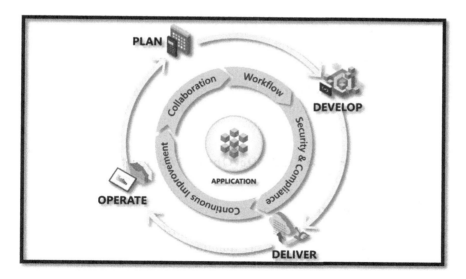

Figure 5.24 DevOps and application lifecycle.

Source: Microsoft portal.

Here are some of points to consider for implementing Zero Trust security in your DevOps pipeline:

- The key principles of ZT such as micro-segmentation, least principle, and Assume Breach security requirements need to be designed in every phase DevOps and its related processes and dependences within the SDLC.
- When working along with third-party vendors and systems, make the Software Bill of Materials a mandatory requirement.
- Do not ignore the need for regular security training and awareness targeting your developers' team.
- Threat modeling practice should be the first step in your SDLC process, which will help identify and mitigate the security risks across your development process on time.
- "Automation" is a key for success; ensure that security tools are well integrated with SDLC to automate the governance with minimum human intervention.
- Integrating Zero Trust into DevOps needs to be based on an adaptive cybersecurity framework that can flex developers' needs while not interrupting how they work best.
- Have strong security threat response management policies to address any security threats if they occur.
- A well-defined access control policies with clear boundaries on access rights, roles, and responsibilities can help to clear conflict between the teams.
- We will see more stringent requirements with personal data security compliance; an organization must design a series of automated audit reporting points to combine DevOps and Zero Trust for better compliance reporting.

For further reading on DevOps Security control, please refer https://docs.microsoft.com/en-gb/security/benchmark/azure/security-controls-v3-devops-security?ocid=AID3044105.

5.13.1 Customer Case Study: DevOps and Application Security with Zero Trust

5.13.1.1 About the Organization

Primarily oriented as a B2B organization specializing in business intelligence for finance and health care. It is an exhibitions, media, and publishing organization, with 10,000 to 15,000 users. It is globally distributed across 40 countries and nearly 150 offices.

5.13.1.2 Current Situation and Current Challenges prior to Zero Trust Implementation

5.13.1.2.1 MERGERS AND ACQUISITIONS

The company would average 22 Merger and Acquisition (M&A) events per year, with a significant amount of IT effort required for each event to first confirm the hygiene of the new company and then consume the new IT infrastructure into the existing environment. This was historically a time-consuming process with great pressure to complete it quickly.

5.13.1.2.2 OFFICE ENGINEERING

A total of 150 globally dispersed offices and a three-year equipment depreciation cycle meant there was a lot of churns for the IT organization. Each office had the typical switch, router, and security stack configuration, and much of the IT staff's time was spent travelling and replacing equipment. Sometimes the company would decide to move the office while resizing instead of replacing equipment causing more work. Internet-only connectivity was the goal to facilitate speed and lower cost for pop up locations.

Significant cloud presence and a desire to adopt multi-cloud. Currently utilizing over 150 cloud accounts and 600 Virtual PC or Virtual Networks. Along with DevOps and quick to market automation workflows meant that the environment was constantly evolving and growing at unpredictable times. It was a challenge to provide consistent protection and monitoring.

- **Worker mobility.** A heavy road warrior workforce meant that consistent security posture was a challenge, particularly in far-flung geographies or over low bandwidth connectivity. Café-style working was an essential goal to deliver a consistent experience and level of protection in any internet-enabled location.

5.13.1.3 Technology Solutions Used for Zero Trust Architecture

Although security was always a concern for the company, it wasn't a motivator to invest in Zero Trust. After discovering the Zscaler platform, the company began planning our Zero Trust transformation journey.

Zscaler presented three major opportunities to the company:

Zscaler' s 100% cloud implementation meant that each office had only general internet connectivity equipment, and our application presentation and security infrastructure were effectively outsourced. This also meant new offices could have their IT infrastructure stood up quickly with very little overhead. As all the offices were isolated from each other, each could have the exact same configuration, down to the subnet of 10.0.0.0/8. We wanted to significantly reduce IT equipment in the offices and reduce the churn through hardware depreciation.

- We wanted to significantly reduce time for IT integration for newly acquired companies. The Zscaler Private Access component meant we did not have to "join" the IT infrastructures together, but users still had the ubiquitous access to all the applications very shortly after the initial M&A event. Applications and data could easily be migrated to the parent company without affecting usage.
- We wanted to rapidly deploy new applications. New cloud locations could also be built quickly and on demand. The ZTA access methods meant there was very little work to deploy new applications for users, since there no firewall or application delivery controller configurations. Deployment times were reduced to hours or days.

5.13.1.4 Top Three Challenges Faced While Implementing New Zero Trust Architecture

- **Application knowledge and migration challenges:** Many applications were old and with staff turnover, and administrative knowledge of some apps was non-existent, so IT staff had to take the lead in migrating from the old presentation method to Zero Trust. Migration challenges included apps that relied purely upon IP addresses and internal authorization mechanisms, which took extra work to integrate Zero Trust solutions.
- **The business case for the transformation:** Significant work was put into producing a solid business case that incorporated the entire cloud/Zero Trust strategy, as individual initiatives did not stand up financially on their own. Much cross-org collaboration was required to receive approval for the project.
- **Staff reskilling programs:** The company had to invest more in its staff in terms of education on cloud and Zero Trust technologies to support the transformation initiative. For example, the network teams suddenly focused on the seven Open Systems Interconnection (OSI) layers, instead of the previous one to three.

5.13.1.5 Impact and Benefits of Zero Trust

- User satisfaction with their working environment improved (measured through surveys and a 40% reduction in ticket rates).
- Speed to provision new offices, datacenter locations and applications, with some improvement changes measured from months to hours.

- Threat detection increased due to the users "always-on" connectivity instead of the internet traffic only being scanned when VPN was turned on.

5.14 Chapter Summary

- A holistic approach to Zero Trust should extend to your entire digital estate – inclusive of identities, user behavior, endpoints, networks, data, apps, and infrastructure. Zero Trust architecture serves as a comprehensive end-to-end strategy and requires integration across the elements.
- Developing for Zero Trust using native cloud tools across multi-cloud environments can be an expensive proposition due to all clouds doing it "differently." For instance, the case study we covered in the hybrid environment using Microsoft and Zscaler technology is one of most required models that many enterprise customers keen to learn.
- A sample architecture for each component or considerations for you to build ZTA architecture to meet your organization's specific needs and technology solutions used for ZTA. Most important, the case studies for each ZTA component session give you great insight and a practical guidance of addressing a business problem.
- Although SOC and DevOps are not necessary to be ZTA components, understanding the importance to follow ZTA model for the SOC and DevOps has become a priority.
- Overall, this chapter has provided enough information for security leadership and architects to plan or develop a ZTA for their organizations.

When it comes to implementing Zero Trust architecture, focus on Progression over Perfection.

Bret Arsenault, CISO, Microsoft

Chapter 6

Zero Trust Project Plan and Program Approach

6.1 The Brave New World

Organizations adapt to three simultaneous transformations at once – **business**, **technology**, and **security**.

Now let's shift to what we see happening to organizations like yours – both the challenges and the bright spots we can all learn from.

Nearly every organization is undergoing top-to-bottom transformation because customers now strongly prefer companies they can rapidly interact with over mobile applications and cloud technologies. This disruption of existing market dynamics forces organizations to transform to compete with technology native start-ups (like Amazon and Uber) and traditional competitors that are digitally transforming.

This **market transformation** kicks off a **digital business transformation** in the organization to capture new opportunities and stay competitive.

This **digital transformation** requires a **technology transformation** for information technology (IT) organizations to integrate cloud services and modernize development practices and related changes to keep up with the rapid market evolution. This should then lead to a **security transformation** that protects these new cloud assets and simultaneously takes advantage of these technologies to manage threats and security risk better.

Unfortunately, security organizations often function as a kind of "last step" quality gate before a release that must justify budget as a particular capital expenditure. This engagement model makes it challenging for security to transform, often causing business and IT stakeholders to skip security to quickly respond to market needs.

Simultaneously, there has been an **attacker evolution** where attackers rapidly adapt to add these new assets to their list of easy targets:

- Attack these lower security workloads that are critical to business growth.
- Find new ways to attack existing assets (both in business models like ransomware and in technical attack techniques).

DOI: 10.1201/9781003225096-9

This creates an increased security risk for new workloads, which attackers take advantage of.

6.2 Working Together as One Team

Everybody must work together during continuous transformations to manage the dynamic market and threat environments; the hallmark of successful organizations that are thriving is that **different teams across the organization are working together** to manage these dynamic challenges. Each team in the organization is undergoing its own massive transformation and figuring it out as they go. Nobody has a clear, detailed, long-term plan that will be accurate in a year.

Recognizing that everyone is adapting to a changing environment will help you better navigate these simultaneous changes:

- **Digital Transformation** – Businesses are constantly reading the market and adjusting plans to ensure they are on the right track.
- **Cloud Transformation** – Technology organizations are constantly working to keep up with the innovation from the cloud providers (for their own efficiency or effectiveness reasons and help enable digital transformation).
- **Zero Trust Transformation** – Security is constantly adapting to the changing threat environment, changing technology platform driven by cloud and, changing attack surface and priorities based on the digital transformation.

To enable this, organizations should build a culture that increases empathy for each other, builds productive relationships, shares context across these disciplines, and encourages learning and collaboration. It's critical for everyone to work together to manage the dynamic market and dynamic threat environment so that the organization stays safe and reduces risk in the time of transformation that we are in.

6.3 Journey to Zero Trust

Zero Trust isn't a thing you buy or "do." Rather, it's a security paradigm and architecture (maturity) journey. As discussed in the previous chapters, the operating model must break down silos and provide unified security across all domains and elements.

To be successful, governance must keep up and drive the right behaviors. To be successful in your Zero Trust project, a detailed roadmap creation is a crucial first step; once the roadmap is clearly defined, it can help business leaders to understand what you are planning to deliver, what investment is required, and what business and security benefits will be achieved out of this project.

To get this big giant called "Zero Trust" out of the room, let's cut down the whole journey into logical project phases or steps (Table 6.1).

Table 6.1 Zero Trust Project Phases

Phase 1: Project Planning and Strategy Consideration
- Phase 1.1: Is Zero Trust project right for you?
- Phase 1.2: Build your strategy and approach using the right Zero Trust framework.
- Phase 1.3: Secure support and buy-in from all the stakeholder.
- Phase 1.4: Identify key interdependencies across the organization.

Phase 2: Zero Trust Maturity Level and Project Roadmap
- Phase 2.1: Build the Zero Trust project roadmap.

Phase 3: Zero Trust Components of the Implementation Roadmap
- Phase 3.1: Create a roadmap to increase maturity for the Identity Domain.
- Phase 3.2: Create a roadmap to increase maturity for the Endpoint Domain.
- Phase 3.4: Create a roadmap to increase maturity for the Application Domain.
- Phase 3.5 Create a roadmap to increase maturity for the Data Domain.
- Phase 3.6: Create a roadmap to increase maturity for the Network Domain.
- Phase 3.7 Create a roadmap to increase maturity for the Infrastructure Domain.
- Phase 3.8: Create a roadmap to increase maturity for the Visibility, Analytics, Automation, and Orchestration Domains.

Phase 4: Continuous Evaluation and Project Monitoring

6.4 Phase 1: Project Planning and Strategy Consideration

6.4.1 Phase 1.1: Is Zero Trust Project Right for You?

Suppose you are moving workloads on the cloud at a rapid pace. In this case, if your organization wants to enable its workforce to work from anywhere, anytime, using any device, you want to take risk-based decisions driven by intelligence-led security. Congratulations! You have made the right decision to adopt the Zero Trust framework. Refer to Chapters 1 and 2 of this book to understand the value and benefits of Zero Trust.

6.4.2 Phase 1.2: Build Your Strategy and Approach Using the Right Zero Trust Framework

This book has referenced several well-documented Zero Trust frameworks that can be used. In determining which might be suitable for your organization, we suggest that you consider these points to help on that decision and plan the journey. The considerations detailed here can be used as a blueprint to shape the overall detailed project plan and tranches and phases.

An element to consider, which is brought to life by this approach, is that is not just about risk reduction alone, and organizations should consider how they maximize return on investment (i.e., achieve bang for buck along the way), allowing them to test and learn and mature over time on this journey.

1. Understand your information assets by both sensitivity (information classification and/or integrity requirements) and criticality (driven by the underlying business process it supports).

   Understanding this enables you to take a risk based, data protection-centric approach to what information assets you prioritize, typically called the "crown jewels." Understanding these highest priority information assets will enable you to be laser focussed as you progress on the other elements that will make up this architecture. For example, not only will identity and device be key, but further sub-dividing the identity and device activity to address the most sensitive information assets first will ensure that you are maximizing risk buy-down and that you are prioritizing finite resources (human resources and dollars) on the highest areas of risk.

   If you don't have a good understanding of this, then this can become a parallel tranche of the plan that enriches the prioritization of activity as you learn this. This doesn't have to be on the critical path but building this out and learning this about your organization will ensure that you are taking data protection-centric, risk-based approach over time.

2. Understand the user population that needs access. For example:

   - Internal users and the org structure – identify high risk users (e.g., traders, payments operators, execs)
   - Third-party supplier user access
   - Contractor access

   This will help inform what populations should be addressed first. Each organization will likely have a different perspective of which user populations they want to start with. Some will start with contractors, some with third parties, and some with internal users. This, coupled with point 1 above, will help organizations start to prioritize activity to ensure the most effective approach is taken with respect to risk reduction and maximizing the use of funds.

3. Identify applications that you want to expose first – start with low-risk applications (derived by the information asset ratings) and determine what will give the biggest business benefit in terms of end user access to applications, for example:

   - entire (or vast majority of) workforce population to email
   - Entire (or vast majority of) workforce population to Intranet
   - Entire (or vast majority of) workforce population to human resources (HR) and personnel applications, etc.

The company should be able to determine this based on existing operational metrics – top 10 applications, applications that have most users access, etc.

This consideration has two benefits. First, it allows the organization to start small with low-risk applications and learn as they progress. Second, it can demonstrate rapid benefits and quick wins, through the measure of consumption, a material uplift of security posture by reaching large populations of the end users.

4. Understand and start grouping key business user populations and core application combinations, for example:

   • Sales teams (users) access to Microsoft Dynamics/Salesforce Customer Relationship Management (CRM)
   • Finance teams (users) access to finance applications
   • Payments staff access to payment systems, etc.

   The company should be able to determine this based on existing business continuity plans, and this will become a key data point for prioritization as well, linking back to the data criticality lens.

5. Start with coarse-grained controls first and refine them over time as you work through the hierarchy of information asset ratings.
6. Overlay additional controls as you work through the user population (pay attention to high-risk users), application risk, device posture, and data sensitivity and criticality. As an example, ensure you have differentiated controls for high-risk users, such as step-up auth, or only certain applications or certain data can only be accessed from corporate managed devices, etc
7. Implement these into policies that can be applied within the Zero Trust ecosystem.
8. Finally, revoke access to previous Virtual Private Network/Remote Access Service (VPN/RAS) services when users have been on-boarded into the above

These points will be underpinned by phase 3 as the next level of detail, which enables the differentiated controls to be applied based on the level of confidence (trust) that has been determined by the risk engine and consequently applied by the security policy engine.

6.4.3 Phase 1.3: Secure Support and Buy-In from All Stakeholders

Everyone has role to play in a Zero Trust project. The Zero Trust project will require new investment or might require a shift in existing invest priorities.

It may trigger change in the role as well organization change. Consider the following points:

- Enforcing strong governance with a Zero Trust approach includes validating business assertions, assessing security posture, and understanding the impact of security culture.
- Identify the key stakeholder from each business unit; also include representatives from legal, HR, the purchasing team, and the admin team.
- Map our roles and responsibility for each stakeholder, identify what support will be required from each of them. For example, executive sponsorship and top-down support from Board members, Chief Information Officer (CIO), and IT Ops team for new or upgrade of IT infrastructure, Enterprise Architecture and target application state for the overall strategy
- Communicate your vision and socialize the Zero Trust project; build awareness on benefits of the Zero Trust project.
- Create the right governance structure to capture regular feedback on the project, share updates, and define a reporting matrix.

6.4.4 Phase 1.4: Identify Key Interdependencies Across the Organization

Zero Trust projects may disrupt many of the existing priorities and projects. In this phase, you must consider the following:

- Revisit the existing business, IT, and security strategy and the impact of the Zero Trust project.
- Identify the list of existing IT, security, and business projects and their interdependencies.
- Identify the key existing requirement for the project that could be disrupted by the Zero Trust project, for example, the authentication requirement for a key business application shared with a third-party contractor or the network micro-segmentation requirement that will impact the new IT Ops project for Microsoft Teams and video conferencing rollout.

6.5 Phase 2: Zero Trust Maturity Level and Project Roadmap

6.5.1 Phase 2.1: Building the Zero Trust Project Roadmap

You will not reach your desired goal or destination if you don't know your current position or maturity level. We have discussed a number of approaches for assessing your current state of Zero Trust maturity in Chapter 3 of this book.

Implementing Zero Trust requires a comprehensive vision and plan, first prioritizing milestones based on the most important assets. Consider the following for building the Zero Trust project roadmap:

- Assess your current Zero Trust technology and controls status; use our maturity assessment model to plot your status or level and set the desired "to be" status or level.
- Set a realistic future status and create a tentative time frame to achieve that status.
- Identify which existing technology and capabilities can be reused for your new Zero Trust architecture (ZTA); for example, one energy company in Australia re-used their existing investment with Microsoft Azure AD and multi-factor authentication technology, which gave them a good kick start in the Identity Domain and reduced the project timeline by almost six months.
- Have a mindset of "think big; start small" – as said by the Microsoft chief information security officer – "Focus on progression over perfection."

6.6 Phase 3: Zero Trust Components Implementation Roadmap

We have discussed the Zero Trust components implementation approach in detail in Chapter 5 of this book. We follow that approach in the required domain to increase the next level of maturity in each of these domains.

Although identity is generally the first domain to consider, it all depends upon the organization's current maturity in each domain. The below list of phases is not in chronological order. You can start any of the domain implementations below unless you have a dependency on another domain; for example, to achieve security maturity in the application domain, you must have a matured identity domain.

6.6.1 Phase 3.1: Create a Roadmap to Increase Maturity for the Identity Domain

Most organizations start the Zero Trust journey with the Identity Domain. Hence, an organization must consider the following to increase the maturity for Identity domain for ZTA.

- Retire the password and go "passwordless." Using passwordless authentication methods such as biometrics, tokens, keys, or Auth-related solutions greatly reduces the surface of man-in-the-middle attacks and threats like Password Spray. Several vendors such as Microsoft, Google, Ivanti, Okta, Secret Double Octopus, Yubico, and others deliver solutions to help organizations move away from the password.

- The "Least Privilege" principle of Zero Trust is an essential factor to consider here. Provide access based on a "need to know basis."
- Few projects such as Privilege Identity Management and Privilege Access Management may be required during this phase to increase your maturity in this domain.

6.6.2 Phase 3.2: Create a Roadmap to Increase Maturity for the Endpoint Domain

After Identity, security of the end user's devices such as laptops and mobile devices is the biggest challenge for the organization. To effectively implement Zero Trust, you must consider the following for this phase:

- Hardening of laptops, mobile devices, and Internet of Things–connected devices
- Having a strong End Point Detection and Remediation solution to have the ability to monitor, isolate, secure, control, and remove the connected device when required
- Applying network segmentation to the managed devices
- Having the ability to enforce security polices on bring your own devices
- Having the ability to automatically remediate threats.

6.6.3 Phase 3.4: Create a Roadmap to Increase Maturity for the Application Domain

To get the full benefit of cloud applications and services, organizations must find the right balance of providing access while maintaining control to protect critical data accessed via applications and Application Programming Interfaces (APIs). Consider the following during this phase:

- Inventory all the applications and API within your organization and apply controls and technologies to discover Shadow IT.
- Have the ability for ensuring appropriate app permission and limiting access based on real-time analytics.
- Have the ability to use cloud-native security controls and managements solutions including monitoring of abnormal behaviors and validating security configuration options.

6.6.4 Phase 3.5: Create a Roadmap to Increase Maturity for the Data Domain

At the end of the day, everything comes back to data security. Take any security framework or standard and the key objective is to protect and secure the organization's "crown jewels," aka the data. The Zero Trust objective is no different. However, data security is not easy, and organizations will be required to evaluate all the pillars and components of Zero Trust together in the context of their key applications, data, assets, and resources.

Consider the following during this phase of the project:

- Understanding of data context, what you trying to protect and why. Where are your data located? Define your date and identify the data, use technologies such as Microsoft Information Protection and eDiscovery, or use Netskope's Advanced DLP to identify and classify the data.
- Understand the value of your data and its lifecycle. Who needs access to the data and why? What protection do you have in place to secure the data?
- Focus on data leakage protection across the entire digital landscape.
- Last but not least, understand the various regulatory, privacy, and compliance requirements which may impact for you data security practices and its maturity such as data disposal and obfuscation requirements.

6.6.5 Phase 3.6: Create a Roadmap to Increase Maturity for the Network Domain

When it comes to the network domain, Zero Trust architecture defines three key objectives:

- Be ready to handle the attacks before they happen.
- Minimize the impact of the damage based on how fast it spreads.
- Make it difficult for the attacker to compromise your cloud resources.

As you continue to define the roadmap for the network domain, consider the following.

- Define your network segmentation strategy.
- Move your workload to different segments based on its criticality and sensitivity.
- Consider security controls implemented to monitor and inspect your "north–south" traffic such as Web gateways, DNS security, application proxy, etc.
- Software-Defined Permitter (SDP), Software Defined Firewalls, and Next-Gen Firewall all now have advanced to support ZTA. Vendors such Netskope, Zscaler, Palo Alto Network, Check Point, and Microsoft provide secure cloud capabilities and secure cloud networks.

6.6.6 Phase 3.7: Create a Roadmap to Increase Maturity for the Infrastructure Domain

In the context of Zero Trust, infrastructure represents an important threat vector to IT infrastructure (on-prem or multi-cloud). Infrastructure includes all the hardware, whether it is physical, virtual, or containerized, including software either open source, first party, third party or software as a service, and microservices (functions, API). The following must be considered during this phase:

- Use of telemetry to detect attacks and anomalies at the infrastructure level
- Assessment of version controls and configuration management
- Administration access control with just-in-time and just-enough access
- Ability to block any unauthorized workloads to be deployed with alert notification
- Data encryption at rest and in motion; and
- Vulnerability scanning and remediation

6.6.7 Phase 3.8: Create a Roadmap to Increase Maturity for the Visibility, Analytics, Automation, and Orchestration Domains

A Zero Trust approach prioritizes routine task automation, reducing manual efforts so security teams can focus on critical threats. Automation is critical to a robust and sustainable security program.

The best Zero Trust deployments automate routine tasks like resource provisioning, access reviews, and attestation. The use of machine learning and artificial intelligence in threat protection tactics through security automation and orchestration enables organizations to defend themselves, containing the attack quickly and ensure resilience of services.

Given the inundation of threat notifications and alerts hitting the Security Operations Center (SOC) today, automation is critical to managing the digital environment at the speed and scale needed to keep up with today's attacks. Consider the following during this phase:

- Provide integrated capabilities to your SOC team to manage threats with the following key abilities.
- Ability to detect threats and vulnerabilities
- Automate the tier 1 analyst investigation
- Automated workflow for responding to the alert
- Manual and automated threat hunting with additional context through analytics
- Ability to prevent and block events in real-time across all the Zero Trust domains.

6.7 Phase 4: Continuous Evaluation and Project Monitoring

Zero Trust is a journey and not a destination; an organization will be required to continually evaluate and monitor the implementation of its ZTA. Several factors may trigger this need of continuous evaluation – it could be the change in business vision, objective, change in treat landscape, change due to regulatory or compliance requirement, change due to advancement in technology, or change due to business merger or acquisition.

It is highly recommended to create program tracks to gauge on the next steps for the Zero Trust program. Program tracks should incorporate the following:

- Program roadmap by track
- Make sure the key stakeholders have continuous visibility by sharing the reports
- Recommendations and the prioritization of the delivery should align with the customer environment
- Create a risk register to capture any blockers during the delivery
- Milestone plan and backlog items (Figure 6.1)

Figure 6.1 is one such example of a scrum framework for a Zero Trust program. Following the scrum framework methodology, an organization can achieve:

- Innovation between teams and business
- Creation of an understanding of the value the program brings to the organization including shared understanding and making complex decisions simpler by doing it in various sprints
- Creation of and building stronger and better organizations
- Tenaciously pursuing the right outcomes
- Aimed to achieve the right organizational goals

Figure 6.2 provides a sample program approach based on this scrum framework.

6.8 Good, Bad, and Ugly – Learnings from Early Adoption of Zero Trust

Zero Trust is a journey, and just like any other digital transformation journey, it comes with its own challenges. The most common challenges include IT, Enterprise access, and security.

IT tasks include users and devices connecting to the internet and intranet. There are varied complexities associated in connecting with modern and legacy

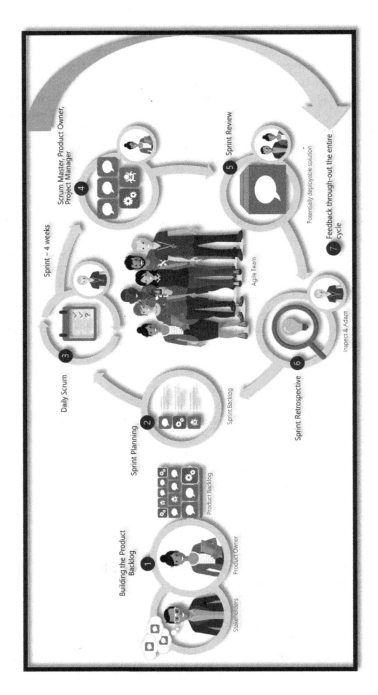

Figure 6.1 Scrum framework for a Zero Trust program.

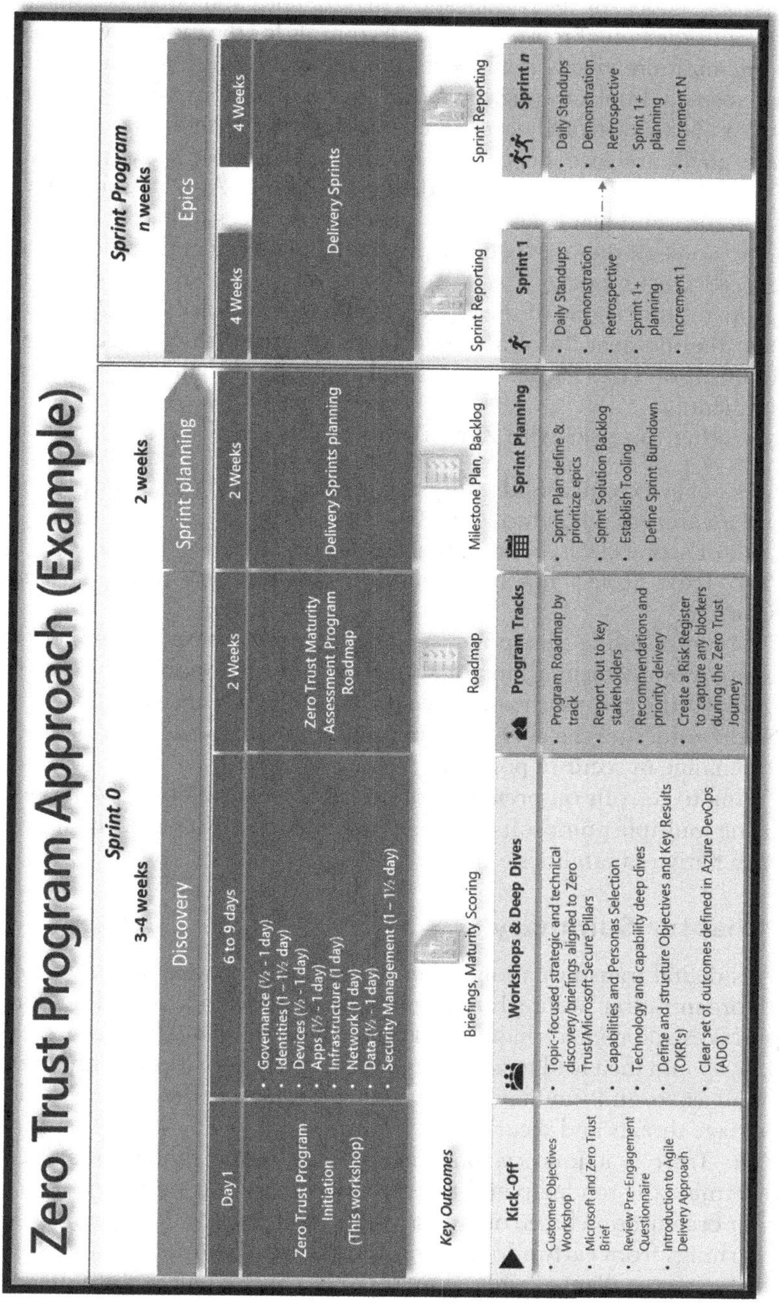

Figure 6.2 Zero Trust Program Approach (Example).

applications. The existing methods are redefined in a Zero Trust approach. The productivity model for an organization may require additional consideration with the introduction of more widespread controls for the modern workplace.

An organization-wide commitment is required for the Zero Trust model to be implemented. Implementing the model may require some short-term urgent decisions to be made in addition to medium- and long-term decision making.

These goals are also dependent on the organization's current state in place for the Zero Trust pillars of Identity, Network, Applications, Devices, Infrastructure, and Data. There may be legacy services linked to all of them or only to some of them, which may affect the planning and implementation of the Zero Trust model.

Interoperability is one of the biggest challenges and risks which can cause a halt in the momentum of a Zero Trust implementation, especially when the organization faces legacy services and application challenges within their environment.

A few other top risks with Zero Trust projects are:

- Lack of key executive and leadership support due to lack of understanding and awareness related to Zero Trust
- Lack of scope clarity among the various organization teams
- Zero Trust project not being aligned with business operation and its priorities
- Overcomplicating the policy engine administration component and trying to implement all major security policies at once
- Ignoring the end-user experience for the sake of security policies
- Not considering the ever-changing threat landscape and not being agile for change in security policies
- Trying to retrofit on-prem security tools to protect cloud workload
- Using multiple point solutions and not considering a platform approach with native capabilities

6.9 Chapter Summary

- This **digital transformation** requires a **technology transformation** for the IT organization to integrate cloud services and modernize development practices and related changes to keep up with the rapid market evolution. This should then lead to a **security transformation** that protects these new cloud assets and simultaneously takes advantage of these technologies to manage threats and security risk better.
- Zero Trust is a journey. Building strategy is the fundamental step to determine the roadmap and the execution steps that matter the most for your organization based on maturity and required Zero Trust components.
- Learnings from early adoption of Zero Trust – Interoperability is one of the biggest challenges and risks which can cause a halt in the momentum of a Zero Trust implementation, especially when the organization faces legacy services and application challenges within their environment.

Modern technology, open architectures and regulatory advances have put Zero Trust at the center of key cyber security advances, supporting the assume breach mindset, enabling continuous verification to enforce least privilege. With the persistence and widespread use of the term, it's critical IT staff understand the core elements to Zero Trust so they can assume the mindset in their own information technology programs.

Chris Hockings, CTO, IBM Security A/NZ

Part 3

Future Horizon of Zero Trust

Trust is a human emotion and is the single greatest vulnerability when we think about cyber security. Given the interconnected and complex world we live in, if we stop assuming a level of trust and start challenging everyone inside and outside of our ecosystem, we can improve security.

Nicola Nicol, **industry expert**

Chapter 7

Future Horizon of Zero Trust

Organizations are all-in with the Zero Trust strategy, and decision makers say it will continue to be the top security priority over the years. Moreover, the relative importance of the Zero Trust strategy as a security initiative is projected to increase by 2023, as security decision makers anticipate that the strategy will remain critical to overall success.

Proving the success of the Zero Trust strategy could fuel further investment. Organizations that have wholeheartedly embraced Zero Trust expect to double down on their investment in the next two years, and those who have not yet started adopting risk falling further behind. These organizations trail their fully implemented counterparts when prioritizing Zero Trust in their security plans and anticipating budget increases and are willing to explore Zero Trust architecture (ZTA) with their new requirements around Internet of Things (IoT) and operational technology (OT) security and governance, compliance, and risk (GRC).

In this chapter, we discuss where ZTA is heading in the future. What priorities can organizations consider when they see an evolution of ZTA in a broader business context?

7.1 Enabling Zero Trust with Artificial Intelligence

Since cloud applications and a mobile workforce have redefined the security perimeter and corporate resources and services often bypass on-premises, perimeter-based security models that rely on network firewalls and VPNs have become obsolete. To address this, vendors like Microsoft developed the Zero Trust Maturity Model to effectively adapt to modern environments' complexities. This provides a massive opportunity for artificial intelligence (AI) powered threat detection services providers to monitor and verify communications to critical business applications. A great example is how Vectra AI partners with Microsoft on Zero Trust Security Framework.

The platform allows security teams to prevent attacks earlier in the kill chain, ensuring that applications essential to business continuity are available and accessible for the entire extended workforce. In addition, Vectra will

DOI: 10.1201/9781003225096-11

help deliver visibility and analytics on the Zero Trust framework's three guiding principles:

- **Verify explicitly.** Always authenticate and authorize based on all available data points, including user identity, location, device health, service or workload, data classification, and anomalies.
- **Use least privileged access.** Limit user access with just-in-time and just-enough access, risk-based adaptive policies, and data protection to protect both data and productivity.
- **Assume breach.** Minimize blast radius for breaches and prevent lateral movement by segmenting access by the network, user, devices, and application awareness. Verify all sessions are encrypted end to end. Use analytics to get visibility, drive threat detection, and improve defenses.

"The Vectra Cognito platform was developed on the idea that standard, static security measures like firewalls, NAC, and VPNs were not enough to protect the modern enterprise," said Randy Schirman, Vectra VP of Partnerships.

Let us go a little bit deeper to understand how AI-powered ZTA is changing the world.

There will be convergence in Zero Trust from security professionals and security services providers to secure devices, data, networks, etc. From a consumer and end-user perspective, there is a need or desire to accomplish similar convergence without compromising their productivity. Organizations try to implement frictionless security, which means they want security and control adopted by the end-users. If the users find that an organization wants to do something beyond their comfort zone, they will find another way to do it much less securely.

This is where possibilities of utilizing AI and machine learning (ML) capabilities for real-time transparent implementation of security and controls have a pivotal role to play. Security and control that we are talking about are not necessarily new. These are the fundamental disciplines of identity, authentication, role-based access control, etc. The mobile users access distributed data from multiple devices, from anywhere. If we implement security and controls that introduce friction to end-user experience, eventually, its adoption will be questionable. Also, business leaders may deprioritize such security and control as it might infringe the end-user productivity. In Zero Trust, the network model is always assumed hostile. Typically, when you apply security and controls on the network, you may tend to believe that we narrow down the perimeter of the network or the segment. In an actual Zero Trust environment, we don't trust the network or any segment.

The policies you apply to users seeking authentication and the resources they are trying to authenticate must be dynamic because the authentication must be derived from multiple sources and not just based on identity, biometric, password, etc. We need various ways to identify who the user is, where they are from, what they are doing, what they want, and what they would likely do when accessing resources. We need to measure all these across the user engagement and lifecycle constantly.

AI can bridge the gap between Zero Trust and zero authentication.

- **Zero Trust** – Security team wants nobody to get or keep access to anything until they prove and continue to prove who they are, that access is authorized, and they are not acting maliciously.
- **Zero Authentication** – End users want immediate gratification with install access to anything and everything they believe they need to get their job done and without hassles of password, timeouts, special permissions, 2nd Factor Authentication (2FA), etc (Figure 7.1).

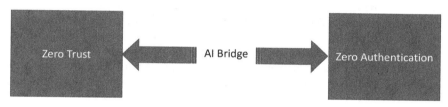

Figure 7.1 AI Bridge between Zero Trust and Zero Authentication

Let us take an example of the Zero Authentication scenario. It is already a big deal for end users to remember a complex password. They usually don't follow setting up a complex password, which is why the password is the number of one threat vector that we need to manage. Because the password is dead, we need a new method of authentication. The new form of authentication would be made possible by user behavior. The measurement and authentication of user behavior would be made possible by ML. We need thousands of user behavior attributes as metrics to ensure user authenticity. ML can verify those thousands of attributes of authentication rules for each user. ML must be implemented in a way that can be real time, perpetual, and continuous.

7.1.1 Role of Artificial Intelligence from Zero Trust to Zero Authentication

- **Contextual Authentication** – AI can help us understand the "macro" context and whether the user's current context fits with trusted behavior and whether we should proceed at all.
- **Continuous Authentication** – AI can help us continuously assess the "micro" context of user's ongoing behavior as it occurs and decide whether we should continue to allow access.

- **Dynamic Policy Authentication** – AI can help us dynamically apply policies in real time. We can allow ML to look at thousands of attributes and use the most appropriate policies for each user. The algorithm can determine these policies for security within ML, so no human intervention is required. We can also allow AI to create a restricted policy based on user behavior concerning the asset, device, or services.

Over the period, ML will learn what is expected (trusted vs. untrusted) for the user, devices, applications, services, etc. Dynamic application of ML will explode the number of characteristics and use cases. You are not necessarily establishing a security program or protocol and telling AI to follow it; instead, what you can do is allow AI to watch your organization's environment and see normal behavior for a productive and secured environment. Providing the visibility of the frictionless environment with reporting would be a massive accomplishment for the management.

There are a handful of software vendors that have achieved significant progress in applying AI in the ZTA. However, recognizing the digital version of individual behavior based on the metadata collected or analyzed by humans or AI should be protected with appropriate privacy and governance. For product vendors, this is the next big step for elevating the maturity of the products.

Organizations that consider enabling Zero Trust with AI must prioritize educating end users about why security policies are applicable for them. Given the threat landscape and ML, we cannot get into a mature security environment unless otherwise security truly becomes part of the organization's culture. When it is part of the culture, the users expect, understand, and are familiar with that their privileges can go up and down.

7.2 Blockchain Technology as Zero Trust Enabler

7.2.1 Blockchain Technology

Blockchain technology is revolutionizing across all industries. As a cryptographic-based distributed ledger, blockchain technology enables trusted transactions among untrusted participants in the network. Bitcoin is the dominant player in the market, followed by Ethereum, Solana, Polkadot, and many others that have emerged with public and private accessibility outside of existing fiat currencies and electronic wallets. Due to its unique trust and security characteristics, industry practitioners, researchers, and application developers have raised significant interest in blockchain technology.

Over the past decade, the popularity of blockchain has significantly increased worldwide. As cryptocurrencies have expanded beyond the worlds of finance and banking, with a slew of new businesses and applications built on the technology, industries now prioritize a mass decentralization that will soon impact the whole world. Blockchain helps distribute the cost of running a platform to its various participants but rewards them for it in equal measure.

The decentralized model is already relevant for blockchain-based solutions such as cloud storage, payment processing, and cybersecurity. There is an upward trend of massive commercial adoption driven by blockchain technology by organizations and cryptocurrency communities. The value of a trustless, decentralized ledger that carries historic immutability has been recognized by other industries looking to apply the core concepts to the existing business processes. The unique properties of blockchain technology make its application an attractive idea for many business areas, such as banking, logistics, the pharmaceutical industry, smart contracts, and most important, cybersecurity.

Blockchain technology shows promises on cybersecurity, and in the recent past, several blockchain security mechanisms have been developed, including access management, user authentication, and transaction security. Due to its prowess in enhancing cybersecurity, blockchain can provide a Zero Trust security framework with highly accessible and transparent security mechanisms via a visible blockchain. All transactions are visible to restricted operators.

If you look at the cryptocurrency ecosystem, blockchain by itself and other vital players such as miners, app developers, exchanges, and decentralized network protocol providers can also leverage ZTA as the foundation of their security architecture (Figure 7.2).

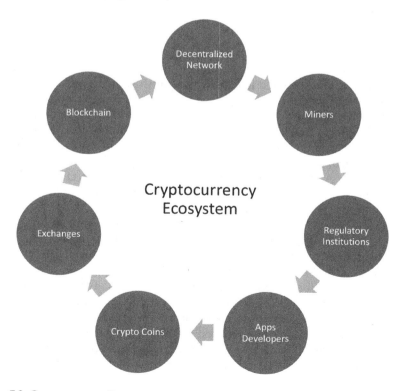

Figure 7.2 Crypocurrency Ecosystem

- **User** – Zero Trust model can be leveraged further by a blockchain due to their sheer immutable nature. Blockchain technology is expected to recognize them, authenticate their trust, and allow them access. Blockchain-enabled Zero Trust security can detect suspicious online transactions, isolate connections, and restrict access to the user.
- **Endpoints (Devices)** – Due to the irreversibility nature of blockchain (everybody has a copy of the ledger), it is hard to use for privacy purposes, particularly in data protection. In current approaches, specific user device preferences are encrypted and stored on the blockchain to be retrieved only by that user. Also, they explore differences between blockchain proof-of-work and proof-of-credibility consensus mechanisms, in which nodes are given a score to determine their credibility depending on the number of connections to other trusted nodes.

  Data between users and applications can be secured and untampered by stored and passing through a blockchain in the decentralized world. Rather than proof of work, trusted nodes are rewarded instead by their calculated trust level assigned by the network. The challenges associated with using security services for blockchain-enabled architecture are authentication, confidentiality, privacy, access control, data and resource provenance, and integrity assurance in distributed networks. This is where ZTA can play a significant role in the following components.
- **Applications (Apps)** – Blockchain security software identifies and addresses the fundamental elements of a cross-industry standard for shared and distributed ledgers while transforming how businesses conduct transactions globally. In the Decentralized Applications (deApps) space, companies can leverage a protected, secure environment for collaboration to develop custom applications and integrate them into existing enterprise systems. In addition, organizations can leverage blockchain's peer-to-peer nature to create internal and external breach-resistant applications for preventing fraud and cyberattacks while managing sensitive data. We will cover more details in the Decentralized Finance (DeFi) section later.
- **Data** – Ensuring that data stored in the cloud remain resistant to unauthorized change, that hash lists allow for searching of data that can be maintained and stored securely, and that data exchanged can be verified as being the same from dispatch to the receipt
- **Network** – Ensure devices and users aren't trusted just because they're on an internal network. Encrypt all internal communications, limit access by policy, and employ micro-segmentation and real-time threat detection. Due to increasingly utilized visualized machines, software-defined networks, and containers for application deployment, blockchain allows for critical authentication data to be stored decentralized and robustly (Figure 7.3).

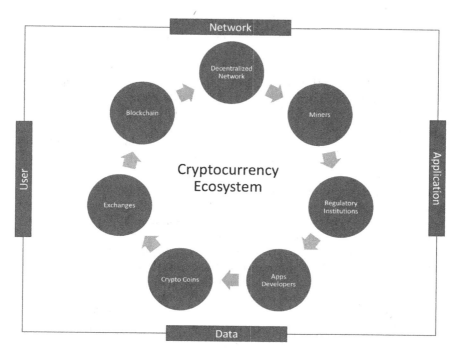

Figure 7.3 Cryptocurrency Ecosystem.

These four ZTA components are foundational to the blockchain-led cryptocurrency ecosystem. As the ecosystem grows and gets more network adoption, the relevance of ZTA will be widely accepted.

7.2.2 Decentralized Finance

DeFi is a blockchain-based form of finance that does not rely on central financial intermediaries such as brokerages, exchanges, or banks to offer traditional financial instruments. Instead, it utilizes smart contracts on blockchains, the most common layer is player is Ethereum. DeFi platforms allow people to lend or borrow funds from others, speculate on price movements on a range of assets using derivatives, trade cryptocurrencies, insure against risks, and earn interest in savings-like accounts. DeFi uses layered architecture and highly composable building blocks.

The concept of DeFi offers an alternative where innovative new financial applications can be quickly developed and easily accessed by all. The right permissionless Distributed Ledger Technology (DLT) network can enable this new era of financial innovation and democratization, providing an open infrastructure of programmable assets that can substantially replace the closed, walled gardens of traditional banking infrastructure today.

The growth of DeFi rests on the shoulders of developers who are building new and innovative decentralized applications to replace traditional and legacy systems. One of the critical barriers that DeFi developers face today is needing a DLT platform that must "reduce smart contract application hacks and failures". Then to accelerate the building of interoperable DeFi apps, an on-ledger system is needed that provides access to modular DeFi "lego bricks".

However, building a reliable financial application is a different class of problem than making a game, web service, or other general application. A DeFi application deployed to a DLT network is expected to run autonomously, trustlessly, and irreversibly while managing millions of dollars in assets. Developers building to specialized requirements like these typically use specialized development environments to make it as easy as possible to avoid bad results.

Developers of DeFi applications need to make sure the code is secure and gets audit approval. The majority of this DeFi application development takes place on JavaScript. Think about the risk factor if the smart contract is open source; anyone can look at the code and manipulate it. A Zero Trust concept must be front and center for robust DeFi security to minimize the risk and improve development productivity. If you're an engineer or developer, build with a Zero Trust mentality, and showcase how we securely modernize our systems and code for your customers.

A new approach is coming in the DeFi application space, having pre-built components of a function or a set of functions developers can leverage to build lego bricks. This can drastically reduce build time and bring them on top of the ledger. In addition, if the DeFi platform providers follow the Zero Trust model across the platform and within the fundamentals of the pre-built components, this will reduce development and audit costs. However, results of penetration tests and network audits carried out from a trustless execution environment would be a helpful bit of information for most enterprise-level smart contract developers, even if they plan to mitigate risk through the aggregation of multiple sources.

7.3 Embracing Zero Trust for the Internet of Things and Operational Technology

The digital workplace means that employees often access their work's network via personal devices, using their home internet or public Wi-Fi. Security protocols must evolve with this change as traditional VPN solutions can grant too much access and expose services to the internet to remote workers, increasing the surface for a cyberattack.

IoT, OT, and network-enabled smart devices all introduce areas of potential compromise for networks and enterprises. As a result, security architects are being forced to re-examine the concept of identity. Many turn to a Zero Trust security model to provide a better architecture in protecting their sensitive resources.

7.3.1 Cybersecurity for the Internet of Things

As organizations continue to drive their digital transformation efforts, especially through the increased deployment of IoT solutions, it quickly becomes clear that the current approach to securing and managing these devices needs to be adapted to the reality of their environment.

IoT solutions need to be secured end to end, all the way from the device to the cloud or hybrid service that the data is processed in. However, securing IoT devices presents a couple of additional layers of complexity because of the incredible diversity in design, hardware, operating systems, deployment locations, and more. For example, many are "user-less" and run automated workloads, presenting challenges when integrating into existing identity and access management tools. Many IoT devices have also been deployed using infrastructure and equipment not initially designed for a connected world or have limited capabilities and connectivity, making them challenging to secure. And because IoT devices are typically deployed in diverse environments – ranging from inside factories or office buildings to remote worksites or critical infrastructure – they're exposed in unique ways and can offer high-value targets to attackers.

IoT solutions have the following technical challenges to consider beyond today's mobile workforce (Figure 7.4).

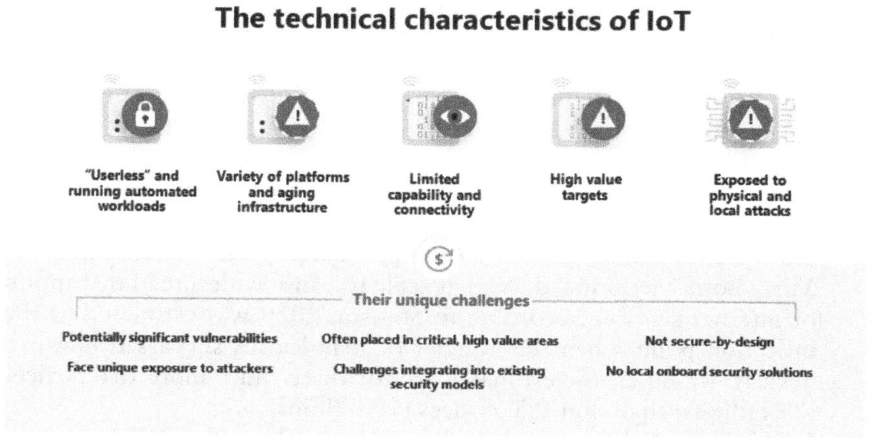

The technical characteristics of IoT

| "Userless" and running automated workloads | Variety of platforms and aging infrastructure | Limited capability and connectivity | High value targets | Exposed to physical and local attacks |

Their unique challenges

| Potentially significant vulnerabilities | Often placed in critical, high value areas | Not secure-by-design |
| Face unique exposure to attackers | Challenges integrating into existing security models | No local onboard security solutions |

Figure 7.4 How to apply a Zero Trust approach to your Internet of Things solutions – Microsoft Security Blog

- IoT devices are" userless" and run automated workloads. IoT devices are often "userless" devices such as cameras, robots, and controllers. In the Zero Trust model for IoT, the "user" of these devices is the device itself acting without human interaction or input. Many workloads running on these devices on edge are automated, deployed remotely as containers, and constantly running to enable critical business processes
- IoT device platforms are varied and integrated into an aging infrastructure. IoT deployments often leverage existing infrastructure made up of aging devices and equipment designed for a disconnected world. Devices run on a mixture of operating systems from bare metal and Real-Time Operating System (RTOS) to rich Operating System (OS) – many with no update capability enabled, often incorporating vulnerable open-source components. There is a proliferation of IoT protocols, often proprietary and unencrypted. Devices can be expected to last more than 10 years, especially when they are embedded in critical infrastructure (such as factories or transportation), potentially exposing them to vulnerabilities for much longer than the PCs and smartphones of the workforce.
- Many IoT devices have limited capability and connectivity. IoT devices can be small, Microcontroller Unit (MCU) class, and may not be capable of running a full OS stack, security agents, or encryption. Limited processing power and size are often paired with the power constraints of running on a battery. Networking topologies can impact the ability to keep devices and workloads managed, up-to-date, and monitored. Constraints can include remote connectivity using high-latency, low-bandwidth cost networks, completely air-gapped installations, industrial-tiered International Society of Automation (ISA)-95 "Purdue model" deployments, and integrated connectivity across cellular, Wi-Fi, and local (such as Bluetooth) stacks
- IoT devices can be high-value targets. IoT devices used in critical operations and infrastructure can make attractive targets as they provide attackers opportunities for command and control that can have real-world impacts, such as the Triton attack. Even when not used for vital operations, the sheer number of IoT devices makes them desirable targets for botnets to compromise at scale. For example, the Mirai Botnet used IoT devices at scale to cause widespread disruption of internet service. According to Statista, 2020 was estimated as the inflection point when the number of IoT devices surpassed non-IoT devices. By 2025, the estimates are for three times more IoT devices (31 billions) than non-IoT devices (10 billions).
- IoT devices can be exposed to physical or local attacks. IoT devices are deployed in environments inside and outside of secured organizational

spaces. For example, a Programmable Logic Controller (PLC) may be installed in a secured factory but is exposed to insider threats from employees or contractors connecting to them via laptops or USB. A security camera or wind turbine may be installed outside and exposed to direct physical attack by adversaries. IoT devices deployed in public spaces such as grocery stores may be connected via networks that the public can locally access.

The ZTA model assumes breach and treats every access attempt as if it originates from an open network. The Zero Trust security model used to protect today's modern workforce, data, and networks can also be applied to IoT in your organization for a holistic security approach. Application of Zero Trust to IoT is important for your organization, given the potential for IoT compromise to cause real business impact.

7.3.2 A Practical Approach for Implementing Zero Trust for the Internet of Things

Securing IoT solutions with a Zero Trust security model starts with non–IoT-specific requirements, specifically ensuring you have implemented the basics to securing identities, devices, and access limits. These include explicitly verifying users, having visibility into the devices they're bringing on to the network, and making dynamic access decisions using real-time risk detections. This helps limit the potential blast radius of users gaining unauthorized access to IoT services and data in the cloud or on-premises, which can lead to both mass information disclosure (like leaked production data of a factory) and potential elevation of privilege for command and control of cyber-physical systems (like stopping a factory production line).

Once those requirements are met, we can shift our focus to the specific Zero Trust requirements for IoT solutions:

- **Strong identity to authenticate devices.** Register devices, issue renewable credentials, employ password less authentication, and use a hardware root of trust to ensure you can trust its identity before making decisions.
- **Least privileged access to mitigate blast radius.** Implement device and workload access control to limit any potential blast radius from authenticated identities that may have been compromised or running unapproved workloads.
- **Device health to gate access or flag devices for remediation.** Check security configuration, assess for vulnerabilities and insecure passwords, and monitor active threats and anomalous behavioral alerts to build ongoing risk profiles.

- **Continual updates to keep devices healthy.** Utilize a centralized configuration and compliance management solution and a robust update mechanism to ensure devices are up to date and in a healthy state.
- **Security monitoring and response to detecting and responding to emerging threats.** Employ proactive monitoring to identify unauthorized or compromised devices rapidly.

Initiating the ZTA process for OT

The first step in adopting Zero Trust access is a proportional security investment that invokes a consistent policy practice of "never trust, always verify". This means protecting every wired and wireless network node to validate all users, applications, and endpoint devices. Arguably, the landscape is complex, but consistent security practices yield protection across all OT systems, whether you're talking about energy and utilities, manufacturing, or transportation. One example is practicing the principle of least privilege across internal and external network communications by providing only the minimally required access and nothing more.

OT system owners can achieve enterprise protection from an array of attack vectors by integrating an internal segmentation firewall at multiple points within the network. In this manner, they accomplish both network visibility and most little privilege enforcement. Additionally, achieving a containment strategy prevents vertical or horizontal movement within the target environment.

Organizations focus on the following needs to lead the future of OT by leveraging the ZTA.

- **Next-Generation Firewalls (NGFWs),** Converged IT and OT enterprises can foundationally build on the ZTA strategy by integrating (NGFW technology that employs an internal segmentation configuration combined with intelligent switching. If the NGFW is configured with secure and scalable Ethernet switches, micro-segmentation and policy enforcement prohibit any east-west or north-south network movement that's not pre-approved. That makes network security more granular while achieving greater attack resistance.
- **Multi-factor authentication (MFA) is another essential cybersecurity practice for OT leaders to enforce role-based access.** With MFA, access is only granted after successfully presenting two or more pieces of evidence, or factors, to an authentication mechanism. These factors may include the following
  - Possessions: things that only the user has, such as a badge or a smartphone
  - Unique identifiers: a fingerprint, voice recognition, or other inherent traits specific to the user

- Knowledge: something that only the user knows, such as a password or a PIN

By requiring several of these pieces of evidence, MFA makes theft and masquerade very difficult to accomplish.

The proportional cybersecurity investment to counter digital transformation and IT–OT convergence risks are hardly about achieving perfect cybersecurity protection. Instead, it is about raising the stakes to the extent that the most critical assets are protected. Typically, sustaining a safe and continuous operation is a top priority, along with deflecting attempts to access intellectual property. For OT, speed, scale, and solution longevity are high-value solution attributes. Despite the best of intentions, it's essential to recognize that cybersecurity attacks fall beyond the detection and scope of ZTA strategy. A distributed denial of service attack, for example, won't show up on that radar.

7.4 Zero Trust in Governance, Risk, and Compliance

Compliance is all about risk management and lessening risk, and the same is true of Zero Trust.

~ *Abbas Kudrati*

GRC is formally referenced as a capability to achieve objectives while addressing uncertainty and acting with integrity reliably. The practitioners in cybersecurity, GRC tools are defined as a measurable apparatus observing policies, regulation, foreseeable issues within the organization, and procedures to manage that entity. GRC refers to a strategy for managing an organization's overall governance, enterprise risk management, and compliance.

- **Governance** is a process through which the executive management ensures the enterprise level policy is adopted at scale.
- **Risk management** is the process of quantifying cyber risk and prioritizing the assessed risks based on their entire operation.
- **Compliance** programs are rules of the market, government, or industry in which the organization operates. This is beneficial to ensuring continuity between organizations in the same field and guarantees a safe, equal playing field for consumers and companies associated with an organization. For example, in the case of cybersecurity compliance, requirements are designed to ensure that consumers can operate within an expected degree of trust in the organization that their data is safe from theft.

This necessitates that risk management aligns with this statement; procedures must be built out to facilitate the "collection of concepts" and to address "per-request access decisions". At the same time, you'll need to add governance and audits to validate the compliance. With these components in place, this increased diligence will reduce your reputational risk, as well as the financial risk of losing money from theft, fines, and revenue loss due to loss of customers.

Adopt an integrated and continuous risk monitoring approach that can uncover hidden patterns, anomalies, threat vectors, and blind spots to proactively monitor and manage third-party risk while considering the changing enterprise risk landscape.

Zero Trust in a way that allows for the dynamic, continuing assessment of risk and that enables the business to continually apply visibility, insight, and action to protect your most valuable assets. Zero Trust also means that we assume we are constantly under attack or compromised and build controls that leverage a threat-centric security architecture.

7.4.1 Zero Trust Is the Best Digital Risk Management Approach

The cybersecurity and compliance experts whose missions support your organization, keep your data safe, and keep your company's name out of the press. But even with such a mission, when it comes to cybersecurity, a worst-case scenario is when a network has been breached, which means the organization's prevention tools failed without notification – known as a false negative – and the company doesn't know the hackers are in.

According to a study conducted by IBM, hackers can reside in your network for approximately eight months before being discovered. During that time, they can steal valuable information.

In an ideal scenario, the incident response team engages quickly and figures out how to prevent the breach from happening again. However, the painful reality is that once the dust settles, the organization may realize that the security products they purchased and implemented could not prevent cybercriminals from entering their network.

If you look at the above scenario from a GRC perspective, here are the observations from this unexpected situation

- **Governance** monitoring missed the hacker.
- Cybersecurity **risk** is now marked RED.
- **Compliance** personnel are running around putting out regulatory fires: privacy breach violation, financial breach violation, etc.
- The C level executives (CxO) and broader members explain the most challenging mitigation plan to improve reputational damage

The shift to hybrid work, accelerated by COVID-19, satellite offices, cloud services, and mobile devices have resulted in networks that are so complex they "[have] outstripped traditional methods of perimeter-based network security as there is no single, easily identified perimeter for the enterprise," according to the U.S. National Institute of Standards and Technology.

A great deal of effort is expended addressing this issue when an uptick in justified paranoia could have significantly reduced the risk. That uptick in paranoia is leading companies to implement proper Zero Trust protocols.

Much like other kinds of digital transformation, Zero Trust isn't a plug-and-play solution to the shortcomings of current cybersecurity practice; it's a total commitment to a process that alters large swaths of an organization's structure.

The organization should consider building a network architecture and resonate and support GRC requirements. Organizations should build procedures to facilitate the "collection of concepts" and address "per request access decisions". In addition, they must also do governance and audits to validate compliance. With these components in place, this increased diligence will reduce your reputational risk, as well as the financial risk of losing money from theft, fines, and revenue loss due to clients leaving.

Like your OS automatic software updates on your mobile devices, industry compliance must be checked to ensure that traffic and assets behave within the industry and organizational compliance rules. Industry compliance checks also cover:

- Threat intelligence feeds, like blacklists
- Malware engine definitions
- Activity logs that can indicate unusual activity

Data access policies such as Data Loss Prevention policies and controls for all unmanaged and managed devices, a Zero Trust system, would be tightly designed and dynamically adjusted for each individual and asset to eliminate lateral movement possibilities for a network intruder. In addition, public key infrastructure that validates certificates issued by an organization to its assets and validates them against a global certificate authority; and security information and event management systems that collect security-related data for extended detection and response services use it for analysis to provide the full potential of the Zero Trust system.

Zero Trust embarks on a significant improvement in digital monitoring (governance), risk reduction, and increased maturity within the compliance framework in the DRM space. In addition, Zero Trust also positively affects the overall maturity of DRM within an organization. Therefore, employing Zero Trust methods and security protocols is the right approach to risk management and the best way to protect your organization.

7.4.2 The Convergence of Data Governance and Zero Trust

In this book, we have explored the need to protect an organization's critical assets by adopting a Zero Trust approach. Digital transformation has fueled the realization that data is the true value creation of an organization and is thus the true critical asset that must be protected. This critical asset resides on-prem and in the cloud, on a CPU that we no longer own, growing at an exponential rate and being accessed by billions of devices. As a result, data enables organizations to gain greater insight into their organization and make smarter business decisions.

Furthermore, consumers are now better informed than ever before and can pick and choose services from competitors. They expect their service providers to understand them, and price services tailored for them. Digital transformation has forced a shift in value from traditional physical distribution channels and legacy technology environments to the scale of customer data and being able to deliver that in a personalized, trusted, and secure way.

As organizations battle to secure this value creation asset to remain competitive, it will become essential for them to adopt robust data governance approaches and ensure that they understand where the critical data (critical asset) resides, how it is accessed, and by whom or by what and what data should be purged and deleted. Zero Trust will fuel this as it will be imperative to minimize the attack surface – these data that reside everywhere being accessed by billions of devices. There will be a mind shift from "addressing and managing an increasing attack surface" to "minimizing the protected surface" by purging no longer needed or relevant data and reducing the burden and complexity of the implementation of a Zero Trust approach. Simplification and industrialization of data governance and Zero Trust will become a symbiotic relationship. Ultimately, there will be a convergence where Zero Trust will form part of a mature data governance approach.

7.5 Chapter Summary

- Organizations that have wholeheartedly embraced Zero Trust expect to double down on their investment in the next two years, and those who have not yet started adopting risk falling further behind. These organizations not only trail their fully implemented counterparts when it comes to prioritizing Zero Trust in their security plans and anticipating budget increases but are also willing to explore and apply ZTA with their new requirements around AI and ML, IoT and OT security, blockchain technology, GRC, etc.

- Possibilities of utilizing AI and ML capabilities for real-time transparent implementation of security and controls have a pivotal role to play. Over the period, machine learning will learn what is expected (trusted vs. untrusted) for the user, devices, applications, services, etc. Dynamic application of machine learning will explode the number of characteristics and use cases. You are not necessarily establishing a security program or protocol and telling AI to follow it; instead, what you can do is allow AI to watch your organization's environment and see what normal behavior for a productive and secured environment is. Providing the visibility of the frictionless environment with reporting would be a massive accomplishment for the management.
- Organizations that consider enabling Zero Trust with AI must prioritize educating end-users about why security policies are applicable for them. Given the threat landscape and machine learning, we cannot get into a mature security environment unless otherwise security truly becomes part of the organization's culture. When it is part of the culture, the users expect, understand, and are familiar with that their privileges can go up and down.
- Blockchain technology shows promises on cybersecurity, and in the recent past, several blockchain security mechanisms have been developed, including access management, user authentication, and transaction security. Due to its promises in enhancing cybersecurity, blockchain can provide a Zero Trust security framework with highly accessible and transparent security mechanisms via a visible blockchain. All transactions are visible to restricted operators.
- The challenges associated with the use of security services for blockchain-enabled architecture are authentication, confidentiality, privacy, access control, data and resource provenance, and integrity assurance in distributed networks.
- In the DRM space, Zero Trust embarks a significant improvement in digital monitoring (governance), risk reduction, and increased maturity within the compliance framework. In addition, Zero Trust also positively affects the overall maturity of DRM within an organization. Therefore, employing Zero Trust methods and security protocols is the right approach to risk management and the best way to protect your organization.

References

- Governance, Risk & Compliance – The CyberGRC Model of Protection | CyberGRC
- Zero Trust is the Best Risk Management Approach | EPAM
- Why Zero Trust Access is Critical to OT Security (automation.com)
- Zero Trust Security Whitepaper_4.30_3pm.pdf (microsoft.com)

- A systematic literature review of blockchain cyber security – ScienceDirect
- How Blockchain is Revolutionizing Content Distribution (investopedia.com)
- Vectra AI Partners with Microsoft on Zero Trust Security Framework – Vectra news release
- Blueprint for Zero Trust in a SASE Architecture, https://resources.netskope.com/cloud-security-solution-white-papers/blueprint-for-zero-trust-in-a-sase-architecture

Index

Note: **Boldface** page references indicate tables. *Italic* references indicate figures and boxed text.

Printed in the United States
by Baker & Taylor Publisher Services